CAPTAIN CARVALLO

A Traditional Comedy in Three Acts

by

DENIS CANNAN

LONDON
SAMUEL FRENCH LIMITED

SAMUEL FRENCH LTD
26 SOUTHAMPTON STREET, STRAND, LONDON

SAMUEL FRENCH INC
25 WEST 45TH STREET, NEW YORK
7623 SUNSET BOULEVARD, HOLLYWOOD

SAMUEL FRENCH (CANADA) LTD
27 GRENVILLE STREET, TORONTO

SAMUEL FRENCH (AUSTRALIA) PTY LTD
ELIZABETHAN THEATRE TRUST BUILDING
153 DOWLING STREET, SYDNEY

MADE AND PRINTED IN GREAT BRITAIN BY
BUTLER & TANNER LTD, FROME AND LONDON
MADE IN ENGLAND

CAPTAIN CARVALLO

Produced at St James's Theatre, London, on August 9th, 1950, with the following cast of characters :

(in the order of their appearance)

ANNI (the Maid)	*Jill Bennett*
SMILJA DARDE	*Diana Wynyard*
THE BARON	*Anthony Pelly*
PROFESSOR WINKE	*Peter Finch*
PRIVATE GROSS	*Thomas Heathcote*
CAPTAIN CARVALLO	*James Donald*
CASPAR DARDE (SMILJA's Husband) . . .	*Richard Goolden*

(Smilja is pronounced " Smeelya ". Winke is pronounced in the German manner, with the " w " as a " v ", and the final " e " sounded. The " e " is also sounded in Darde. In Carvallo the second " a " is short, as in " valley ".)

SYNOPSIS OF SCENES

The action of the play passes in the kitchen of the Dardes' farmhouse, on disputed territory, during the last summer of a long war

ACT   I   Evening
ACT   II   A little later the same evening
ACT III The early hours of the next morning

To face page 1—Captain Carvallo

CAPTAIN CARVALLO

ACT I

SCENE.—*The kitchen of the* DARDES' *farmhouse, on disputed terri-tory. An evening during the last summer of a long war.*

The kitchen is large, airy and comfortable, with plaster walls and timbered ceiling. A door C. *of the back wall leads to the farmyard and main road, with a distant view of the mountains beyond. An arch down* L. *leads to the dairy and a door down* R. *to the parlour. There are casement windows* R. *of the door up* C., *in the side wall up* R. *and in the side wall up* L. *A stair-case leads off* R. *to the upper rooms. A large tiled stove with a wide chimney over it fills the wall* L., *between the arch and the window. A large cupboard is built-in under the staircase* R. *There is not much furniture. A dresser stands* L. *of the door up* C. *and a small cupboard stands under the window up* L. *A set of bookshelves hangs on the wall above the fireplace. There is a small elbow chair below the stove and a large elbow chair stands* R. *of the stove. A kitchen table with a small chair* R. *of it stands* L.C. *The only floor covering is a rush mat in front of the stove. The dresser shelves have the usual complement of plates, mugs and bowls, while shelves over the stove carry the cooking utensils. There are plants in pots on the inner window-sills and on the top of the pelmet of the window up* L. *A row of hooks* R. *of the door up* C. *is hung with aprons, jackets and other garments. Bright curtains hang at the windows. An old-fashioned, battery-type radio receiver stands on a low shelf* R. *Farm baskets and water jars are stacked under the upstage end of the staircase. Bundles of onions and herbs hang from a beam. A small mirror hangs on the staircase rail up* R. *At night the room is lit by an oil lamp on the table.*

(See the Ground Plan and Photograph of the Scene.)

When the CURTAIN *rises the door up* C. *is closed, and the stage is empty.* ANNI, *the maid, enters immediately down* L. *She is aged nineteen. She carries a broom, but is in no mood for work. She wears a national costume with full skirts almost to her ankles. She crosses to the wireless and switches it on. The aria " How Strange and Dead " from " The Bartered Bride " is heard from the wireless.* ANNI *moves to the door up* C., *opens it then leans against the doorpost and gazes off* L. *to the mountain view as she listens to the music. After a few moments she sees someone coming in the distance, moves* R.C. *and hastily begins to sweep.* SMILJA DARDE *enters up* C. *from* L. *She wears a becoming national costume with full skirts almost to her ankles and the frill of a petticoat showing underneath. She carries a basket of gooseberries which she puts on the table. She then gets an apron from the hooks up* R. *and puts it on. For a few moments she stands and listens to the music.* ANNI *leans her chin on the broom, and they both forget themselves and each other in a dreamy enjoyment. There is a pause in the song, and they unwillingly relax. Then, to disguise her feelings,* SMILJA *speaks unnecessarily sharply.*

SMILJA (*moving below the table*). What are you doing?

ANNI. Sweeping. (*She sets to work.*)

SMILJA. Well, don't raise all the dust like that. How often have I told you to wet the floor before you sweep?

ANNI (*leaning her broom against the staircase*). I'm sorry, Mrs Darde. (*She picks up a small jar of water from under the stairs.*)

SMILJA. And turn off that wireless.

ANNI (*protesting*). Oh . . .

SMILJA. Turn it off, I said. It makes one dream, instead of working.

(ANNI, *with bad grace, switches off the wireless.*)

ANNI (*starting to spatter the floor down* R.C. *with water*). Did you hear the guns just now?

SMILJA. No. Did you?

ANNI. Yes—ever so clearly.

SMILJA. Well, they must have been a long way off if I didn't hear them.

ANNI. You don't hear things so well when you get to your age.

SMILJA. My age! How old do you think I am?

ANNI. Fifty.

SMILJA. Fifty! You haven't heard anyone say I was fifty, have you?

ANNI. No. I just guessed. (*She replaces the jar under the staircase.*)

SMILJA. You'd better stop guessing people's ages, until you're either experienced enough to guess right, or wise enough to guess politely.

ANNI (*picking up the broom*). How old are you, then?

SMILJA. I'm only . . . Never you mind.

ANNI. I shall be twenty next month. It's a turning point, you can't deny it. (*She sweeps, then stops.*) How old is Mr Darde?

SMILJA. If you want to know, you ask him.

ANNI. I did. And he said " a hundred and three ", and smacked me on the bottom.

SMILJA. Serve you right.

ANNI (*very confidentially*). I say : where is Mr Darde ?

SMILJA. He's gone to Velma to buy some manure. Now get on with your sweeping, and don't skimp the corners.

ANNI. He may have gone to Velma, but not to buy manure. Mrs Darde : he's a Partisan, isn't he ?

SMILJA. You should know better than to ask questions like that.

ANNI. I'm sorry. (*She sweeps determinedly.*) D'you think the war will be over this summer ?

SMILJA. I expect so.

ANNI. Oh, I hope not.

SMILJA. You don't mean to say that you enjoy the war ?

ANNI. What girl in these parts wouldn't ? Dull as a ditch, this place was, until the call-up. Then all the village boys went, and those nice Dragoons came.

SMILJA. They were a rowdy lot of ruffians.

ANNI. You had the major to tea—every Sunday.

SMILJA. That was different.

ANNI. Why ?

SMILJA. He was an officer.

ANNI (*sweeping up* C.). He wasn't any different when it came to the corn merchant's daughter. (*She stops sweeping when she comes to the door up* C.) Peace—all the village boys will be home again, with their bent backs and their spotty faces, begging one to marry them.

SMILJA. You'll be glad enough one day when you get a proposal.

ANNI. I shan't marry till I'm thirty.

SMILJA. That's what I said.

ANNI. How old were you when you did marry ?

SMILJA. Twenty-five.

ANNI. Why didn't you and Mr Darde have any children ?

SMILJA. Because not everybody does. And your mind is always running on the same subject. You must try to think of something else.

ANNI. What did you think of, when you were nineteen ?

SMILJA. Well, of course I thought of men sometimes, just as you do. But I also thought of other things like—like botany, and God.

ANNI. Botany ! The lady who taught us botany at school called buttercups *ranunculi*, as though she was afraid to use their christian names. As for God—well, He . . . Why do we call Him He, and not she or it ?

SMILJA. Anni dear ! You . . .

ANNI. Well, I want to *know*. I know quite a lot about men, and so they're interesting to think about. But I don't really know anything at all about God, and so He's boring.

SMILJA. You don't know anything about God—and I taught you all about Him for five years in the Sunday school! You know everything that's necessary to make you a good religious girl, don't you?

ANNI. No.

SMILJA. No?

ANNI. If God doesn't want me to think about the things I do, why does He put the thoughts into my head?

SMILJA. He doesn't. The Devil does.

ANNI. Then why do we pray to God: " Lead us not into temptation? " We ought to say that to the Devil.

SMILJA. I'm sure I gave you a little book which explained all this quite clearly. There's no need for you to bother your head about such things.

ANNI. But you just said I *was* to—to keep my mind off the other thing.

SMILJA. The best thing for you to do now is to sweep the floor, and that'll keep your mind off everything.

(ANNI *starts to sweep by the door up* C., *then looks off* L.)

ANNI (*after half a stroke with the broom*). There's the Baron. He's coming into the yard.

SMILJA. The Baron! Are you sure?

ANNI. Yes. He's coming in here.

SMILJA (*crossing hurriedly to the mirror* R.). Put away the broom. (*She tidies her hair.*) And fetch some wine and some glasses from the parlour.

(ANNI *crosses to the door down* R., *watches* SMILJA *for a moment, then sniggers.* SMILJA *turns indignantly.* ANNI *exits down* R. *The* BARON *enters up* C. *from* L. *He is aged fifty and bald. He is dressed in an old-fashioned shooting costume and wears a haversack. He carries a double-barrelled shotgun.*)

BARON. Aha! Don't think I didn't see you at the mirror. Who were you dolling yourself up for, eh?

SMILJA (*crossing below the table*). Certainly not for you, Baron.

BARON (*pursuing* SMILJA *unsteadily* R. *of the table*). That's the way you always go on—bridle up the minute you're paid a compliment—raise your eyebrows till they fall off the back of your head—wriggle and jiggle like a bashful girl in a hayfield— oh, you prim, ripe plum of a Sunday school marm, you . . . (*He misses the seat of the chair* R. *of the table, and sits abruptly on the floor down* C.)

SMILJA (*easing down* L.). Baron—you're drunk!

BARON. Praise be to the blessed saints, I am tight as a tick. I brought you a rabbit. (*He rummages in his haversack and takes out a rabbit.*)

(ANNI *enters down* R.   *She carries a bottle of wine and two glasses.*
SMILJA *signs to* ANNI, *who waits down* R.)

(*He dangles the rabbit.*)   There you are!   A fine, plump, tender
young buck.   (*He tosses the rabbit on to the table.   He sees* ANNI.)
Wine!   Do I see wine?

SMILJA.   No—now, Baron, you mustn't.

BARON.   You are right.   Take it away.   I have reached the
exquisite equilibrium of intoxication.   One more glass would
make me vicious, and two would make me sick.

(ANNI *exits down* R.)

SMILJA (*sitting in the chair* L. *of the table*).   Are you sober
enough to tell me what's happened to my husband?   (*She
begins to remove the stalks from the gooseberries.*)

BARON.   I can only tell you that he's been sent on an important
mission.

SMILJA.   Is it dangerous?

BARON.   Of course it is.   It's damn dangerous to be a Partisan
at all—you know that.

SMILJA.   When will he be back?

BARON.   Perhaps this evening.

SMILJA.   Thank goodness.

BARON.   Perhaps—one must face it—never.

SMILJA.   Oh!

BARON.   But should that happen—should the worst occur—
you know that there's always someone who—who would . . .
Oh, dammit!   I'd like to think myself a blunt kind of chap
who always says what he thinks.   But when I hear myself saying
what I think I'm thinking, I never think it sounds a bit like
what I've thought.   But you know what I mean.   Don't you?

SMILJA.   I'd rather believe that you're drunk, and making a
fool of yourself.

BARON.   You're too good for all this.   Sunday school teaching,
and churning milk, and—and shelling gooseberries.   Married to
a dreary dog of a dissenting lay-preacher . . .

SMILJA.   If you go on like this, I'll have to make you go.

BARON.   Yes!   That's right—turn me out of the only place
where I can get a bit of homely comfort and intelligent conversation.

SMILJA.   You're not very good company this evening.

BARON (*picking up his gun*).   I'm a damn sight better company to you than I am to myself.   In another five minutes
I'll be sober, and then me and myself will hardly be on speaking
terms.

(ANNI *enters hurriedly down* R.)

ANNI.   He's coming.

SMILJA (*rising*).   What?

ANNI (*moving to the window up* R.). Mr Darde—he's coming up the lane.

SMILJA (*moving to* ANNI *and looking over her shoulder*). I don't see him.

ANNI (*pointing off* R.). There! You can see his hat—bobbing along behind the hedge.

SMILJA (*turning and moving* R.C.). Oh—thank heavens—he's safe!

(ANNI *moves to the door up* C. *and stands outside it looking off to* R.)

BARON (*moving down* L.). Well, I must push off.

SMILJA. Don't you want to wait and see Caspar?

BARON. I'm his commanding officer, and I refuse to grant him an interview when I'm in no fit state to command. I'll look you up later. I'll . . . (*He sees that* ANNI *is watching for* DARDE *outside the door*.) I don't like him to think that I'm always hanging around the place. You know why, don't you?

SMILJA. If you're going, go. I've a lot to get ready.

BARON. All right, all right—there's no need to be so horrible to me. I'll go to bed and read the advertisements in last week's paper. All the things that were for sale are sold, so I can't buy anything and I'll save money.

(*He exits quickly down* L. SMILJA *goes up the stairs.*)

SMILJA (*on the stairs*). Anni—bring up the kettle. Did you put out a fresh cake of soap when you did the room this morning?

ANNI (*moving to the stove*). Oh, no—I forgot. (*She picks up the kettle and crosses to the stairs.*)

SMILJA. One of these days I'll forget to pay your wages.

(SMILJA *and* ANNI *exit at the top of the stairs.* PROFESSOR WINKE *appears outside the window up* R., *peers in, then enters cautiously up* C., *moves to* R. *of the table and looks around the room. He wears a very ill-fitting suit of agricultural clothes.*)

(*Off.*) Get a clean towel from the drawer.

ANNI (*off*). Which drawer?

SMILJA (*off*). The bottom one, of course, silly.

(WINKE *retreats towards the door up* C. *He is just going out as* SMILJA *enters and comes down the stairs.*)

Caspar! Caspar, I've been so worried. Wherever in the world have you been?

(WINKE *stops and turns.* SMILJA *screams.*)

WINKE. Now please—please don't be alarmed. Please be calm, and listen to what I tell you. I promise you there is a perfectly simple explanation.

(ANNI *enters at the top of the stairs, sees* WINKE *and screams.*)

Oh, my God! If anyone else is going to come in and do that, will they please come quickly and get it over? My nerves are really in no state for these dreadful demonstrations.

SMILJA. Who are you? What are you doing here? And why are you dressed in my husband's clothes?

WINKE (*moving down* C.). I am Professor Winke, of Velma University. I am dressed in your husband's clothes for the very simple reason that he is wearing mine. And I hope he finds them better fitting and cleaner than I do his.

(ANNI *comes down the stairs.*)

SMILJA (*moving to* R. *of* WINKE). Where is my husband? Tell me—nothing dreadful has happened to him, has it?

ANNI. He hasn't been arrested for being a Partisan?

SMILJA (*turning to* ANNI). You've finished for the day—go up to your room.

ANNI. Oh, whenever anything interesting happens, I'm always packed off upstairs.

SMILJA. Will you do as you're told?

(ANNI *goes up the stairs and exits.*)

WINKE. Now, may I first bother you for something to eat? I haven't had a bite since breakfast.

SMILJA. You can eat when you've told me what you've done with my husband.

WINKE. You know that he was to be sent on a mission?

(*The sun sets and the light begins to fade.*)

SMILJA. Yes.

WINKE. Well, so was I. We were to start from the same place. Just before our departure I became—rather violently indisposed. It made me quite unfit for the task that had been set me—overhearing a conference of enemy officers by concealing myself in a cupboard. So it was decided that I should perform your husband's task—which only entailed a brief journey with despatches, by corridor train—and he should carry out mine. My task could only be done by someone looking like a city man, and his by a person of countrified appearance. So we had to change our clothes. Until he returns, from the enemy's point of view, I am a farmer and lay-preacher, and he is a Professor of Biology.

SMILJA (*moving above the table*). Well, even if that's so, why did you have to come in here and frighten us like that? (*She transfers the rabbit and gooseberries to the dresser.*)

WINKE. Because your husband's mission was to finish in this house.

SMILJA. You're to meet someone here ?

WINKE. Yes. Though I don't know whom. (*He sits in the chair* R. *of the table*.)   Now, might I bother you again for something to eat ?

SMILJA (*moving to the dresser*). How long have you been working for the Partisans ?   (*She gets two plates, a knife, a fork and the cruet from the dresser and sets them on the table.*)

WINKE. A fortnight next Tuesday.

SMILJA. Is that all ?   My husband's been with them for over two years.

WINKE. Really ?   But then he joined them for romantic reasons, and I for realistic ones.

SMILJA (*moving to the cupboard up* L.). What do you mean ? (*She gets a piece of boiled ham, some cheese and a loaf from the cupboard and sets them on the table.*)

WINKE. As he appears to be a very religious person, I imagine he joined for the pleasure of slaughtering the unrighteous—like a crusader setting forth to slay the infidel.   I joined because I happen to be the greatest living authority on what is vulgarly called the tadpole.

SMILJA. Whatever have tadpoles got to do with Partisans ? (*She carves some slices of ham and puts them on* WINKE's *plate.*)

WINKE.   After the war is over, there will be a dreadful snobbery about what one did in it.   Unless I help to blow up a few of the enemy, I shall find myself called a collaborator, and no-one will let me get near to a tadpole for the rest of my life.   What is worse, all the work I've already done would be discredited, because political tact is much more important nowadays than scientific accuracy.   (*He cuts a slice of bread.*)   So, I'm putting in a few months of rather amateur work with a cloak and dagger, in the hope that the witch hunters and purgers will leave me in peace.   (*There is a short pause as he starts on his meal.*)   This is excellent bread.   Do you bake it yourself ?

SMILJA. Yes.

WINKE. How very foolish. You had much better run a communal bakery for the village. Every woman would thus save an hour a day.

SMILJA. What would she do with it ?

WINKE. The bread ?

SMILJA. No, the hour.

WINKE. Improve her mind.

SMILJA. How ?

WINKE. Have you no facilities for adult education ?

SMILJA. No.

WINKE. Disgraceful. You'd better start some classes.

SMILJA. Where ?

WINKE. I don't know. Have you no public buildings ?

SMILJA. Only the church.

WINKE.   Just the place.   There will always be plenty of room.

SMILJA.   I thought so—you're an atheist.   (*She prepares the table-lamp.*)

WINKE.   Yes.   The first you've met ?

SMILJA.   No.   But the first who wasn't ashamed.

WINKE.   Why should one be ashamed of what one believes ?

SMILJA.   You are proud of what you don't believe.   That is something quite different.   Have you a match ?

WINKE.   Why do you go to the trouble of bringing oil all the way from Persia, when by sticking a windmill on the roof you could do everything by electricity ?   (*He takes a box of matches from his pocket and hands them to* SMILJA.)

SMILJA.   Why are you making a meal of my cold ham, when by bringing a packet of vitamin pills you could have fed yourself, and left nothing to wash up ?

WINKE.   Ah—because I *enjoy* cold ham !

SMILJA (*lighting the lamp* C.).   I enjoy lighting the lamps, and keeping them clean and shiny.

WINKE.   You're absurdly old-fashioned.   If you had all that brasswork scientifically treated, they would only need a wipe once a year.

SMILJA.   Did you say you were a professor ?

WINKE.   Yes.

SMILJA.   Does that mean that you teach people ?

WINKE.   Yes.

SMILJA (*moving above the table*).   No wonder the world's in such a mess.

(ANNI *enters by the passage and comes down the stairs.*)

(*To* ANNI.)   Where are you going ?

ANNI.   Out.

SMILJA.   Where to ?

ANNI.   Just—out.

SMILJA.   Who are you meeting ?

ANNI.   No-one in particular.

SMILJA.   Well, don't go hanging round the camp where the enemy soldiers are.   I won't have it.

ANNI.   It's nothing to do with you.   You're not my mother.

SMILJA.   It was through your mother hanging around camps after the last war that you came into the world.   And I don't want to see history repeating itself.

ANNI (*getting her coat from the hooks up* R.).   It's so silly to talk of them as " enemy soldiers ".   Some of them only come from forty miles to the east of us.   (*She puts on her coat.*)   Just because they were born the other side of a wire fence, it doesn't make them any different, does it ?   They speak the same language as we do, don't they ?   Only they have a much nicer accent, and *I* think much nicer manners.

SMILJA. That doesn't alter the fact that they're our enemies. Moses and the Midianites only lived a few miles apart; but that didn't prevent Moses from being good, and the Midianites from being bad; and Moses went up and smote them, and serve them right. So don't go near the camp, or when the village boys come back they'll shave your head.

ANNI (*moving to the door up* C.). Well, I'd sooner be bald myself than have a bald admirer.

SMILJA. What do you mean?

ANNI. *Good* night, Mrs Darde.

(ANNI *exits up* C. *to* R., *closing the door behind her.*)

SMILJA. That girl . . .

WINKE. Don't worry. At the moment she's a near traitor. In a couple of years' time all the politicians will be saying exactly the same things—for the wrong reasons. By the way, what's your Christian name? I should know—just in case.

SMILJA. Smilja.

WINKE. Smilja. And I'm—Caspar. Caspar Darde.

SMILJA. You're not going to pretend to be my husband? (*She returns the box of matches to* WINKE.)

WINKE. I have his identity papers, and he has mine. So if we happen to meet any of the enemy I'm afraid it's unavoidable.

SMILJA. I wish Caspar would come. It's getting so late. Are you married yourself?

WINKE. Of course not.

SMILJA. Why—of course not?

WINKE. As a bachelor, I can regard the tadpole objectively. Suppose I get married, and breed like my subject, the frog; can I still regard the reproductive process as a chemical reaction, achieved with the aid of a reflex, and directed by some crude signpost, like the blue behind of an ape, or the bull-frog's *basso profundo*? No! The only mind that can be truly objective is the mind that is wholly pure. No man capable of love is fit to think. I therefore maintain that . . .

(*There is a loud knock at the door up* C. WINKE *rises.*)

SMILJA. That's not Caspar. (*She moves up* R.C.) And none of the neighbours would knock like that. Go upstairs . . .

WINKE (*crossing below the table to the stove*). It's too late. Whoever it is will have seen me through the window. You forgot to draw the curtains.

SMILJA (*looking through the window up* R.). It's an enemy soldier! (*She turns.*) What are we to do?

WINKE (*getting the newspaper off the cupboard up* L.). The trouble about speaking the same language as the people you're fighting is that you can't pretend not to understand them. I'm afraid I must depart from all my principles, and behave like a married man. (*He sits in the chair* L. *of the table, puts his feet up on the stove and opens the newspaper.*)

(*There is another knock.* SMILJA *opens the door up* C. *and steps back as* PRIVATE GROSS *enters. He is a soldier burdened with a great deal of equipment, including a portable bath and a small canvas bucket in which a geranium is growing.*)

GROSS.   Is this the house of Caspar Darde, farmer ?

SMILJA (*easing down* R.).   Yes.

GROSS.   Thank God. (*He lets his equipment and the bath cascade to the ground, and puts the geranium carefully on the table.*) They told us it was only a few hundred yards. More like half a mile it was. (*He looks out of the door up* C.) Where's he got to now ? (*He calls.*) Sir ! Here we are, sir. Sir !

(CAPTAIN CARVALLO *enters up* C. *from* R. *He is aged thirty. He wears a bedraggled but well-cut uniform, with muddy field boots and breeches.*)

CARVALLO (*as he enters*).   There's no need to shout, Gross. I was looking at the moon.

GROSS.   I'm sorry, sir.

CARVALLO.   I should hope so. (*He moves* C. *to* SMILJA.) Good evening. My name is Captain Carvallo. I'm sorry, but I have to requisition a room ; and a dog basket or something for my batman. Would you mind showing him where to put my things ?

SMILJA.   We're very short of rooms at the moment. We . . .

CARVALLO.   According to the billeting notice you have three bedrooms.

SMILJA.   Yes. But the servant girl has one . . .

CARVALLO.   And do you and your husband sleep apart ?

SMILJA.   Oh—no. But we're expecting a visitor.

CARVALLO.   Who ? I ask because I would naturally give way to an invalid or an elderly person.

SMILJA.   No, it's—well, it's the Professor of Biology at Velma University.

CARVALLO.   Really ? I had no idea that I should meet such distinguished company in a farmhouse. When is he arriving ?

SMILJA.   Perhaps tonight—or perhaps not for a day or two. He's extremely old, and he suffers from sciatica.

(*There is an indignant rustle of* WINKE'S *newspaper.*)

CARVALLO.   Well, let's hope I'm still here when he comes, and we can have an interesting chat—that is, if you have some-where else you can put me ?

SMILJA.   I'm afraid not.

CARVALLO.   I saw a stable across the yard, with a loft over it. The loft should be fairly empty at this time of year ?

GROSS. For God's sake let's get settled down somewhere. I was up at half-past four.

CARVALLO. Will you stop mumbling and muttering, Gross? I'm quite sure we can both settle ourselves very nicely in the stable. Go and see if it will do, and be careful of the geranium.

as script (GROSS *mutters and picks up his kit.*)

What did you say?

GROSS. Nothing, sir. But you've more kit to go about with than any other officer I've ever had. (*To the others.*) I ask you—a geranium.

CARVALLO. It's a very rare species that I rescued from a bombed botanical garden. I've conquered three countries with that geranium, and I'm not parting with it now. Go and put up my bath.

—in fact Bath GROSS. Bath. I wonder you don't carry round a turkey [Turkish] carpet and a four-poster bed.

CARVALLO (*moving above the table*). Don't be insolent, Gross!

GROSS. I wasn't being insolent, sir. (*He picks up the bath.*) I was paying you the compliment of treating you like a civilian.

X I T.   (*He exits up* C. *to* L.)

CARVALLO (*putting his geranium on the window-sill up* R. *among the other flowers*). Now, I haven't had a bath for nearly a fortnight. I can provide anything else, if you can heat me some water. Oh, and I wonder if I could possibly borrow a pair of sheets? You've no idea of the luxury they'd be for me.

SMILJA. You can have them—so long as you have a good bath first.

CARVALLO. Splendid! And I'll help myself meanwhile to a little bread and cheese—my rations will be round in the morning. You don't mind? (*He sits in the chair* R. *of the table.*)

(SMILJA *exits down* R. *and leaves the door open.* WINKE *is still behind the paper.*)

(*To* WINKE.) It's a wonderful thing how international the maternal instinct is. I find I can get almost anything anywhere by simply looking young and rather tired.

(WINKE'S *newspaper is immobile.*)

Do you mind if I exercise my privilege as the occupying power, and ask you to draw me some water?

(WINKE *rises angrily, puts the paper on the cupboard up* L., *then crosses to* R. *and looks around for the tap.*)

WINKE (*calling*). Smilja!

SMILJA (*off*). What is it?

WINKE. Which tap shall I get the water from?

(SMILJA *enters down* R.)

SMILJA.   What did you say, dear?

WINKE.   What tap shall I get the water from—dear?

SMILJA (*pointing to the arch down* L.).   The pump in the dairy, of course.   There's a pan beside it, *dear.*

(*She exits down* R.)

WINKE (*crossing to the arch down* L.).   I hope you understand that this has nothing to do with paternal instinct.

(*He exits down* L.   CARVALLO *rises, nibbling a piece of cheese, warms himself at the stove, and then turns to look at the books on the hanging shelf.*   WINKE *re-enters down* L.)

That pump is ineffective.   No water comes up.

CARVALLO.   Excuse my asking, but are these your books?

WINKE (*crossing below the table*).   Um—yes.

CARVALLO.   How very interesting.   I didn't know that any-one still read this sort of thing.   *The Lost Lamb, or Strayed from the Fold.   Little Gems from Galilee.*   I mean—one only finds that sort of thing nowadays in secondhand bookshops.

WINKE.   More is the pity.

CARVALLO (*moving to* R. *of the stove*).   Yes.   Yes—I quite agree. But it's refreshing to find someone who still retains the old sense of values.   Tell me—I'm interested in all men's beliefs—do you find your faith adequate to modern conditions and events?

WINKE.   Entirely.

CARVALLO.   Do you, for instance, believe in evolution?

WINKE (*after a mental struggle*).   No.

CARVALLO.   You believe that man and woman were created exactly as described in the book of Genesis?

WINKE.   I do.   Wholeheartedly.

CARVALLO.   So you think that all biology is so much nonsense?

WINKE.   Certainly.   It is the great heresy, foretold in the book of—somewhere.   All biologists should be burned at the stake.

CARVALLO.   Then why on earth is a Professor of Biology coming here to stay as your guest?   You haven't lured him along to set him alight?

WINKE.   No.   No—I am going to convert him.

CARVALLO.   That should be worth seeing.   I hope I'm still here when you do it.

WINKE.   I hope not.   The struggle of a biologist trying to stop believing he's descended from a monkey, and begin believing he's descended from a man, is a sight most painful to behold. They are frequently seized with convulsions.

CARVALLO.   You have converted a good many of them, then?

WINKE.   Quite a few.   I make quite a business of it.

B

CARVALLO. Then, Mr Darde, I would be most grateful for your help.

WINKE. What?

CARVALLO. I came at an early age under the influence of a science master—a rabid materialist—who taught me to believe in nothing, because if I did so I would never be disappointed. I find now that believing in nothing disappoints me every minute of the day. I see the stars on a frosty night, I fall in love with a woman, I'm in ecstasies at the music of a band—and I find it dreadfully disappointing to think that women and stars and music are only molecules and energy and illusions in my mind. I'm the saddest young man in the world, because I understand the principles of everything, and if someone or something doesn't mystify me soon I really think I shall go mad.

WINKE. I'm afraid I'm rather full up with conversions at the moment. I've a long waiting list. If you like to come back after the war, perhaps I'll be able to fit you in.

CARVALLO. Oh, but . . .

WINKE. I was going to point out that the pump isn't working. I'm afraid you'll have to do without your bath.

CARVALLO. But I must have a bath—I'm filthy. Surely we can find out what's wrong with the pump?

WINKE. I know exactly what's wrong with it. Owing to a contraction in the circumference of the plunger, the partial vacuum in the cylinder is non-existent, and as the pressure in the pump equals that on the water surface, the water obeys the normal principles of hydraulics and fails to rise.

CARVALLO. Thank you. But what are we to do about it? I want a bath.

(SMILJA *enters down* R. *She carries some bed linen.*)

WINKE. Dearest, the pump won't work.

SMILJA (*moving to the door up* C.). I expect it's the washer. Pour a jug of water in at the top.

(*She exits up* C. *to* L.)

WINKE. A jug of water? The necessary vacuum will thus be created by . . . Ah, yes! I see! (*He crosses to the arch down* L.) A most ingenious application of Bellamy's law. I should never have thought of that.

NTER (*He exits down* L. GROSS *enters up* C. *from* L. *He carries a packet of cigarettes.*)

GROSS (*moving above* CARVALLO). I brought your cigarettes.

CARVALLO (*taking the cigarettes*). Thank you. What's it like? (*He puts the cigarettes in his pocket.*)

GROSS. Cushy billet. (*He nods after* SMILJA.) She's a good looker, isn't she?

CARVALLO. Yes.

GROSS. You, or me?

CARVALLO. Me.

GROSS. I thought so. She said something about a servant girl. Me?

CARVALLO. I'll let you know when I've seen her. One of them is bound to be virtuous—you can have her. I think this part of the war's being rather fun, don't you?

GROSS. For you it is. Since the last advance, one grocer's wife, one assistant matron, two school teachers and a waitress.

CARVALLO (crossing below the table to R. of it). We'll forget about the waitress.

GROSS. Why?

CARVALLO. I'm not a lecher, Gross. I'm a lover.

GROSS. What's the difference?

CARVALLO. You're a realist, Gross, and I'm a romantic. Or rather, that odd modern mixture—the materialist who craves romance. That's what makes our conversation so intriguing.

(WINKE enters down L. He carries a pan of water.)

Gross—give him a hand. (To WINKE.) You know, you're very slightly built for a farmer. You look more like the academic type.

WINKE (putting the pan on the stove). Fasting has made me thin. I'm still suffering from Lent.

CARVALLO. Oh. Your wife, if I may say so, is a very fine looking woman.

WINKE. A not uninteresting example of a well-defined ethnic type.

CARVALLO. Have you any children?

WINKE. Not as far as I know.

CARVALLO. What?

WINKE. Ah—not—no. Will you excuse me?

(He exits down L.)

GROSS. Sounds fishy to me. Either she isn't his wife, or she's a three-legged rabbit.

CARVALLO. What's a three-legged rabbit?

GROSS. Easy to catch.

(SMILJA enters up C. from L.)

CARVALLO. Now go and put up my bed, Gross, will you? And here we're far enough back to wear pyjamas.

GROSS. The silk or the wool?

CARVALLO. The silk.

GROSS. D'you want your hot-water bottle?

CARVALLO. Of course.

X I T

(GROSS *exits up* C. *to* L., *and closes the door behind him*.)

SMILJA (*moving above the table*).   Have you finished now?
CARVALLO.   Yes, thank you.
SMILJA.   Don't you say grace?
CARVALLO.   I don't know how to.   As a child I would have
said "Thank God for my good supper".   But as I no longer
believe in any God, that would be hypocrisy.   Won't you say a
grace for me?
SMILJA.   I couldn't do that, because your religion is not the
same as mine.   (*She starts to clear the table, puts the food in the
cupboard and the dirty plates on the dresser*.)
CARVALLO.   I have no religion.   What is yours?
SMILJA.   We are dissenters.
CARVALLO.   Oh.   From which church do you dissent?
SMILJA.   We dissent from all churches.
CARVALLO.   But you must have a church of your own?
SMILJA.   Yes, but we call it a Tabernacle.
CARVALLO (*crossing to the chair* L. *of the table*).   Do you mind
if I sit by your fire for a moment?   These early summer evenings
can be chilly.   (*He sits*.)   Oh, this is nice and peaceful.   Do you
know what one longs for, more than anything else, when one's
up in the line?
SMILJA.   No.
CARVALLO.   A warm kitchen and a woman making things tidy.
SMILJA.   You can talk, can't you?
CARVALLO.   It's a change from giving orders.
SMILJA.   I'm sorry you've come to such a bad billet.
CARVALLO.   Have I?   It seems the best I've had for years.
SMILJA.   I mean that there's only one young woman here,
and she's gone out for the evening.
CARVALLO.   Did I say that she must be a young woman?
Young women bore me to tears.   No-one is the least interesting
until they're in their thirties.
SMILJA.   How old are you?
CARVALLO.   I was thirty yesterday.
SMILJA.   Well now, have you warmed yourself?   You're sit-
ting in my husband's chair.
CARVALLO.   I thought it fitted me astonishingly well.
SMILJA.   It's always the same with soldiers.   They kill your
relations and drive their tanks across the crops, and then they
turn round and make pretty speeches to the girls.
CARVALLO (*rising*).   But that's exactly the romance of warfare.
SMILJA (*moving to* R. *of the table*).   Romance!
CARVALLO (*standing with his back to the stove*).   Yes—romance!
Look at me: seven years ago I was going to be a draper in a
one-eyed little town where the girls were the plainest you ever
saw.   I suppose I'd have married one of them, for want of a

better, and by thirty-five I'd have been a fat tradesman with an ugly family selling celluloid collars and worrying over the mortgage. Instead, I've travelled in a dozen countries, I've put an inch on my chest and taken two off my waist, I've a hundred and twenty men to command, a personal servant and a car. I've had far more spare time than I would ever have had as a draper, and in it I've developed a taste for music and literature, and seen far more famous cathedrals and architectural wonders than I would ever have seen as a civilian. In my kit-bag I've two etchings by Rembrandt, that I bought off a hungry dealer in your capital for a pound of dripping. In peacetime, I could hardly have afforded the frames to put them in.

SMILJA. You're an officer, and the war's going well for you. What about the others?

CARVALLO. What others? Look at the girls in your own village street, mixing with all manner and races of men, instead of the few half-witted hayseeds who courted them in peacetime. Look at you and me; we'd never have met, if six years ago someone hadn't marched across a frontier. Can you honestly say that you're not glad we've met, when we're getting on so famously?

SMILJA (*moving to* L. *of the table*). I don't call it getting on when one person's making long speeches, and the other's tidying the kitchen.

CARVALLO. Forgive my saying so : but did you know that you have a grey hair?

SMILJA. Nonsense. Where?

CARVALLO. May I pull it out for you? (*He moves to* L. *of* SMILJA.) Stand still. (*He pulls a hair from her head.*) There! (*He turns and puts the hair quickly into the stove.*)

SMILJA. I don't believe it was grey at all.

CARVALLO. I promise you—almost white.

SMILJA. Then why did you get rid of it so quickly—so that I shouldn't see?

CARVALLO. Would you like me to find you another?

SMILJA. You couldn't.

CARVALLO. I'll bet you I can. I saw another. Stand still. (*His eyes are not on her hair at all, but are covertly watching her profile.*) No. I can't find it. Perhaps because I don't want to.

SMILJA (*not moving*). Do you try this—wherever you stop for the night?

CARVALLO (*also quite still*). No. On my word of honour, no.

SMILJA. How much is your word of honour worth?

CARVALLO. When I give it to a man, a bishop's oath on the Bible. But when I give it to a woman, I must candidly confess that its value varies.

SMILJA (*turning her head to look at him*). Why?

CARVALLO. Because any man would swear anything in the world for such favours as you could grant him.

SMILJA. In all my life—I've never had such a thing said to me. But you don't mean it. You've said that sort of thing a dozen times before.

CARVALLO. I've said it a hundred times before. But this is the first time I've meant it.

SMILJA (*moving below the table to* C.). Then if you've always told lies until now, how can you be so certain that you're sincere all of a sudden ?

CARVALLO (*moving to* L. *of* SMILJA). Because—although being alone with a beautiful woman on a summer's night is a situation I'm perfectly used to—this time, I'm a little bit frightened. I feel clumsy, and awkward and quite at a loss. When one loses confidence, one is most likely to be sincere.

SMILJA. Why am I letting you talk to me like this ? I must be out of my mind.

CARVALLO. Getting out of one's mind is the most important of all human activities. Why don't we both go out of our minds together, and have a splendid surreptitious holiday ?

SMILJA (*retreating to the stairs*). How dare you ! If you mean what I think you mean, I can't possibly speak to you again. (*She goes hurriedly up the stairs and stops on the first landing.*) I've never had a holiday in my life, and I don't need one. And *my* mind is a very comfortable place, and you've no right to come bursting in and—and . . .

CARVALLO (*moving to the foot of the stairs*). Bursting in and disturbing it.

SMILJA. You're not disturbing me at all. You couldn't disturb me. I'm a married woman, and I'm old enough to be your—your elder sister.

(*She goes up the remainder of the stairs and exits.* CARVALLO *sighs, eases* C. *and lights a cigarette.* ANNI *enters up* C. *and closes the door behind her.*)

ANNI. Oh—good evening, Captain.

(CARVALLO *takes no notice.*)

(*She moves to* R. *of* CARVALLO.) I was out for a walk. (*She crosses below him to the stove as she takes off her coat.*) Then I heard that some soldiers had come in here, (*she moves up* C.) so I came back to see if I could help. (*She hangs her coat on the hooks.*)

CARVALLO. M'm.

ANNI. Are you staying here ?

CARVALLO. What ? Yes.

ANNI (*moving to* L. *of* CARVALLO). I work here, you know.

CARVALLO. Oh.

ANNI. I live here too.

CARVALLO. Really.

ANNI (*desperately*). Are you *tired*?

CARVALLO. Yes. Extremely.

ANNI. I thought you must be. Oh, well, it's nice to see a new face for a change. The shortage of man-power here is awful. Not that the village boys were ever much to write home about. A bit soft in the head most of them were. They say it's something to do with the water.

CARVALLO. You ought to be ashamed of yourself.

ANNI. Me? Why?

CARVALLO. Don't you realize that I'm your enemy? Where's your patriotism?

ANNI. I say—you're not a padre, are you?

CARVALLO. No. I'm sorry if I seem unresponsive. I can assure you it's the first time in my life that I've failed to seize such a tempting opportunity.

(SMILJA *enters at the top of the stairs.*)

(*To* SMILJA.) Ah—you've come back!

SMILJA (*coming down the stairs*). I've come back because I heard you talking to Anni.

CARVALLO (*ironically*). Oh?

SMILJA. And because you are not a fit person for young girls to associate with. Anni—go up to your room.

ANNI. So that's what's up, is it?

SMILJA. Go along, you little wretch! And wash your neck —it's been dirty all day.

(ANNI *flounces upstairs and exits.* SMILJA *moves to the dresser and looks in the drawers.*)

CARVALLO. What are you looking for?

SMILJA. My knitting.

CARVALLO. Can I help? What sort of knitting?

SMILJA. A grey sock.

(*They both look for the knitting.*)

CARVALLO (*looking in the least likely places*). Are you going to knit upstairs?

SMILJA. Yes.

CARVALLO. Have you got a fire up there?

SMILJA. No.

CARVALLO. It must be rather cold, isn't it? Why don't you knit down here?

SMILJA. Because you're here. And I don't want to talk to you.

CARVALLO (*moving down* R.). It wouldn't be in any of the cupboards, would it?

SMILJA (*moving down* L.). No.

CARVALLO (*moving* C.). But there's no fire in the stable, and I'd be dreadfully cold out there.

SMILJA. You've got a hot-water bottle, haven't you? Go off to bed.

CARVALLO. Why don't we call a truce, and sit down comfortably by the stove and talk about ourselves?

SMILJA (*moving up* L.). Because I doubt if there's anything you could say about *your*self that would be fit for me to hear.

CARVALLO (*crossing to the chair down* L.). It wouldn't be behind that cushion, would it?

SMILJA. No! I've looked.

CARVALLO (*lifting the cushion*). Where's your husband?

SMILJA. I expect he's writing a sermon.

CARVALLO (*producing the knitting from under the cushion*). Here it is.

SMILJA. Where was it?

CARVALLO. Behind the cushion.

SMILJA. Oh.

(CARVALLO *stands holding out the knitting, waiting for her to come and take it. As she does so, he holds it and doesn't let go.*)

CARVALLO. Now—if I give it you, will you come and sit down?

SMILJA (*tugging the knitting away from him*). I wish you had never come here.

(*He places the chair* L. *of the table for her.* SMILJA *sits, and begins her knitting.*)

CARVALLO (*sitting in the chair* L.). And you said that you would never speak to me again.

SMILJA. We very seldom see people here. It makes a change to have a talk with a stranger sometimes—any stranger. I'm not paying you compliments.

CARVALLO. Even if the stranger's your enemy?

SMILJA. One reads books and listens to music written by one's enemies.

CARVALLO. Your books seem to me to be written entirely by your own countrymen, and exclusively by priests.

SMILJA. Those are my husband's. I have a library of my own—but you mustn't mention it to him.

CARVALLO. A secret library? What do you keep there?

SMILJA. You promise not to say anything? I read—novels.

CARVALLO. Oh.

SMILJA. *French* novels.

CARVALLO. Oh dear. Well, this is the last thing I expected.

SMILJA. Why ?

CARVALLO. Your—mask—is so very convincing. (*He rises suddenly.*) I'm sorry. (*He crosses to* R. *of the table.*) I behaved a few minutes ago as I'd behave to any comely farmer's wife I met in the course of my travels. I insulted you by underrating your intelligence—and your worth. I'm really rather upset about it. I promise you I will now behave myself properly.

SMILJA. You'll find it rather cold over there. The stove doesn't throw out much heat.

CARVALLO. Thank you ; but I'm not used to living indoors. I find it rather warm.

SMILJA (*after a pause*). You are quite forgiven for anything you said.

CARVALLO. But I upset you. You were really quite shocked and . . .

SMILJA. Oh no, I wasn't. I'm quite used to that sort of thing.

CARVALLO. You are ? In novels, you mean.

SMILJA. No. In railway carriages.

CARVALLO. Oh.

SMILJA. And I should be hypocritical if I pretended that I shall not be a little disappointed when the time comes when I shall always be treated with respect.

CARVALLO. I suppose that even to the most virtuous woman it must be a bit of a wrench when virtue ceases to be a chosen state, and becomes a pathological condition. (*He switches on the wireless.*)

SMILJA. Are you the Devil ? You certainly talk like him.

CARVALLO. Not so far as I know. (*He selects some soft music.*)

SMILJA (*after an awkward little pause*). Have you to go in the morning ?

CARVALLO (*crossing above* SMILJA *to* L. *of her*). Yes, I shall probably have to go tomorrow. Or perhaps an orderly might come for me now, and I'd only have time to say good-bye. Well—don't look so sad about it.

SMILJA. I wasn't !

CARVALLO. I wonder if people ever live and love as intensely and magically in peacetime as they do in war. I don't know. I was still a boy when war broke out. But you were a woman. Do they ?

SMILJA. I've always been too busy trying to keep up with the housekeeping to bother about whether I was living intensely or not.

CARVALLO. And loving ?

SMILJA. I don't know what you mean. A woman like me marries the man of her choice and settles down with him. You talk as if you fell in love every fortnight.

CARVALLO. But I do !

SMILJA. What ?

CARVALLO (*kneeling* L. *of* SMILJA). I mean—no ! No—I am often strongly attracted to a woman ; my fancy gets to work on some pretty face I've seen in passing. But I don't think I've ever really fallen in love, as one says, before.

SMILJA (*capturing a lost stitch with great concentration*). I have always understood that falling in love is a thing one cannot prevent. But if such a thing happens to one, especially if the circumstances make it wicked, one should keep it to oneself and not mention it.

CARVALLO. And are you really angry with me because I did mention it ? Can you honestly say that you don't feel happier and younger, and that the world isn't full of far more beautiful things, now that I've told you that I love you ? You're looking twice as lovely. And your knitting's getting in an awful tangle.

SMILJA. It's nothing to do with you—I'm not very good at knitting. And the world looks exactly the same as it did.

CARVALLO. You know, I can't help feeling that while I'm behaving like a scoundrel in telling you the truth, you—for the best of motives—are telling me the most enormous lies.

SMILJA. Oh—I'm not !

CARVALLO. You're blushing, your voice is unsteady, your hands are trembling, and you've just changed from plain to purl in the middle of a row.

SMILJA. Will you please stop interfering with my knitting.

CARVALLO. Then will you please tell me that you're not angry, and that you don't regret that I said what I did ?

SMILJA. Everything that I've ever been taught, or learned to believe, tells me that you are behaving in a very wicked and irreligious manner.

CARVALLO (*rising*). And so are you.

SMILJA. I am not.

CARVALLO. You are. (*He crosses below the table to* C.) You ought to have stayed upstairs, instead of coming down here for your knitting. That old sock gave me hope. Without it, I would never have opened my mouth.

SMILJA. Very well, then. I admit that I should have stayed upstairs.

CARVALLO. Good ! Then we are both being wicked ?

SMILJA. Yes. But you far more so than me.

CARVALLO. It's a polite pretence that the man always is. Well, that at least is a beginning.

SMILJA. There cannot be any such thing as a beginning when there is no possibility of an end.

CARVALLO. Oh, do for heaven's sake stop it ! (*He switches off the wireless in a temper.*)

SMILJA. Stop what ?

CARVALLO. You seem to have no idea of how to misbehave

yourself at all.   Anyone would think you were a Sunday school teacher or something.

SMILJA.   I am !   And I have been for fifteen years.

CARVALLO.   Good Lord !   Then I'm getting on better than I thought.

SMILJA.   And it seems to me that you turn everything upside down.   Most people expect a woman to be good.   Really I'm beginning to think you'd be happier with the corn merchant's daughter.

CARVALLO (crossing down L.).   Oh, let me admit it, then : I'm a scoundrel, a cad, a bad type—the sort of young man you wouldn't trust with your sister.   But like the very worst of scoundrels, I sometimes surprise myself longing secretly for righteousness.   I'm not yet a total loss, and I would dearly like to find a good woman who would save me.   (He moves to the stove.)   You wouldn't like to take me on, would you ?

SMILJA.   No, I would not !

CARVALLO.   Oh, why ?

SMILJA.   Because—because in saving you, I might be in danger myself.

CARVALLO.   You might ?   Oh, how wonderful !   This is a declaration !

SMILJA.   It's nothing of the kind.

CARVALLO.   Of course it is—it must be.   Oh, I haven't been so happy for centuries !

SMILJA.   You are deliberately misunderstanding me.

CARVALLO.   You can't go back on what you said—you said I was dangerous to you.

SMILJA.   You shouldn't want to be.   I don't believe you want to be saved at all.

CARVALLO.   I do !   And how can I be saved, except by the love of a virtuous woman ?

SMILJA (putting her knitting on the table).   A virtuous woman wouldn't find you dangerous—I'm as wicked as you are—how can I save you ?

CARVALLO.   Then we must save each other—what a delightful prospect.

SMILJA (rising ; angrily).   You've only one idea in your head. First you make eyes at me.   Then, when that fails, you try to get round me by wanting to be saved ; and then, when you've put me in a muddle so that I don't know whether I'm still good or worse than you, you offer to save me from yourself.

CARVALLO.   You're going to burst into tears at any moment.

SMILJA (stamping).   I'm not !   (She breaks below the table.)

CARVALLO.   You are !   Please go on—it's the best possible thing.

SMILJA (tearfully).   It's not !   It makes me look perfectly dreadful.

CARVALLO. Then do it. It might save both of us.

SMILJA. Oh! I think you're outrageous! (*She bursts into tears.*)

CARVALLO. Ah—thank goodness! (*He moves in to* L. *of her.*) There's nothing like salt and water for making a woman reasonable. (*He puts his arm around her.*) Now come and sit down, and let it all come out in a good wet rush.

SMILJA. I want—I want a handkerchief.

CARVALLO (*turning her to face him, so that his arm encircles her*). Here you are. (*He takes his handkerchief from his pocket and gives it to her.*) It's not very clean, but that makes it all the more absorbent.

(WINKE *enters down* L. *He moves to* L. *of them unnoticed and has to tap* CARVALLO *on the shoulder before they separate.*)

WINKE. Oh—hullo. You couldn't let me have a cigarette, could you?

CARVALLO. What did you say?

WINKE. I've run out of cigarettes. You haven't got any, have you?

(*In great amazement,* CARVALLO *takes a packet of cigarettes from his pocket and offers them to* WINKE.)

(*He takes the packet.*) Thank you very much. Oh—that water of yours ought to be hot by now. I'll give you a hand to take it over. (*He puts the packet in his pocket.*)

(SMILJA *eases* C.)

CARVALLO. Thank you. I'm not making a mistake, am I? You are this lady's husband?

WINKE. Yes, that's right. I'm her husband, Caspar Darde. What! Oh, *yes*! Here, by Jove, I say—I forgot! What the flaming devil were you doing with my wife when I came in? Eh? Explain yourself you—you—you—you . . .

CARVALLO. Ah, thank goodness! This is a situation I can understand. (*With practised fluency.*) Sir: I apologize. The whole thing was entirely my fault. When a man has been at the front for some time you will understand that his susceptibilities are considerably increased—increased to the point of his sometimes making a fool of himself. On a sudden inexcusable impulse I grabbed your wife round the waist and embraced her. That is all there was to it.

WINKE. Oh. I'll take your word for it. But mark my words, and don't let it happen again.

CARVALLO. No, sir.

WINKE (*shaking hands with* CARVALLO). Thank you very much. (*He crosses below* CARVALLO *to* L. *of* SMILJA.)

CARVALLO. I think you put my cigarettes in your pocket.

WINKE. So I did. (*He takes the packet from his pocket and gives it to* CARVALLO.) Awfully sorry. My dear Smilja, I admire the fortitude with which you have suffered the advances of this low fellow, and I sympathize with your very natural tears. (*He clasps her awkwardly to his chest.*) There, there, it is all over, and your husband is here to protect you.

(CASPAR DARDE *enters abruptly up* C. *He is cross and hot. He wears an ill-fitting morning suit and carries a brief-case and umbrella.*)

SMILJA (*breaking to* R.). Caspar!

DARDE (*moving between* SMILJA *and* WINKE). Why—you abominable scoundrel! What are you doing with my wife?

He raises his umbrella to belabour WINKE *as—*

the CURTAIN *falls.*

ACT II

SCENE.—*The same. A little later the same evening.*

When the CURTAIN *rises,* CARVALLO *is holding a Court of Inquiry. He is seated imposingly above the table, on which are various forms and papers.* GROSS, *armed with a rifle and bayonet, stands at ease* R. *of the table.* WINKE *and* DARDE *are seated on chairs set formally down* R. *of the table.* DARDE *is below* WINKE. SMILJA *is seated down* L. *of the table. There is a pause, while* CARVALLO *finishes writing, then he lights a cigarette, and looks searchingly at* SMILJA, DARDE *and* WINKE *in turn.*

CARVALLO. Very well—so the story you ask this Court of Inquiry to believe is as follows : Mr Darde—the real Mr Darde —goes to the funeral of his aunt in Velma. Having no suitable clothes, he borrows some from a friend of his—a friend with the improbable name of Professor Winke. Urgently requiring some legal papers relating to his aunt's estate, he unexpectedly returns home—still wearing the improbable professor's clothes, and inadvertently carrying the professor's identity papers, which that absent-minded and improbable gentleman has left in the pocket. Correct ?

DARDE. That is, I should say, the substance of what occurred.

CARVALLO. But is it true ?

DARDE. Young man, it is not permitted to mere instruments of Providence like ourselves to declare what is true and what is false.

CARVALLO. But this is a Court of Inquiry !

DARDE. I do not recognize the jurisdiction of any Court of Inquiry, except that Court that shall be called on the Day of Judgement.

CARVALLO. Well, we really can't adjourn until then.

DARDE. I will say, however, that the summary of events you have just given appears to me, an ignorant and doubtless mis-guided observer, to correspond with what—apparently—occurred.

CARVALLO. Thank you. Now you, being also absent-minded —like the professor—had left your identity papers behind here ?

DARDE. So it would seem.

CARVALLO. Returning, you find in your house a despicable creature who has purloined *your* identity papers and is wearing your clothes, and is apparently taking advantage of your absence to enter into guilty relations with your wife ?

DARDE. That was the impression I formed.

26

CARVALLO. You agree that that is a fair summary of the events of the last twelve hours ?

DARDE. A reasonable person might suppose so.

CARVALLO. Then please sign this statement in quadruplicate. I am satisfied that you are the real Caspar Darde, and that this lady is your wife.

(DARDE *rises, moves to the table, signs the document then resumes his seat.*)

I am not at all satisfied as to this improbable Professor Winke, who lends out clothes in Velma, and I shall get our intelligence to verify his existence. But the most mysterious feature of the case is the gentleman beside you—if, indeed, we can call him a gentleman. (*To* WINKE.) Who and what, may I ask, sir, are you ? And now that we have exposed your fraud in using Mr Darde's papers, where are your own ?

WINKE (*rising*). I can best explain the reason why I have no papers by stating that I am an anarchist. I disapprove of all regimentation, documentation, and indeed of all organization of anything whatever—*in toto.* You ask what I am. I am a wandering scholar. You ask who I am.

CARVALLO. I do.

WINKE. My name is—Legion.

CARVALLO. Legion ?

WINKE. Yes.

CARVALLO (*writing*). What are your christian names ?

WINKE. Primus, Secundus, Tertius.

CARVALLO. Mr Legion—are you trying to make a fool of me ?

WINKE. Your creator has already done so.

CARVALLO. Gross, will you point your bayonet at a tender part of Mr Legion's anatomy.

(GROSS *prods* WINKE *with his bayonet.*)

You say that your names are Primus Secondus Tertius. I've heard of successive members of a family being named after the order of their arrival : but surely no-one can arrive first, second and third ?

WINKE. I arrived on the first day of the second month in the third year of this century.

CARVALLO. Ah—I see. Gross, you may now allow the gentleman to stand easy.

(GROSS *lowers his bayonet.*)

Now, what are you doing in this house ?

WINKE. You have already given a possible explanation.

CARVALLO. Is it the true one ?

WINKE. It's the only one I can think of.

CARVALLO. Had you met Mrs Darde before ?

WINKE.   No.

CARVALLO.   When did you arrive?

WINKE.   This afternoon.

CARVALLO.   And you mean to tell me that you had reached that degree of intimacy with Mrs Darde by nightfall?

WINKE.   The word " intimacy " has a special legal connotation which I cannot accept.   I had my arm round Mrs Darde's waist. That, in law, is familiarity, it might be assault, but it is not intimacy.

CARVALLO.   Are you suggesting that Mrs Darde's character is such that a perfect stranger, after a few hours of acquaintance, would be permitted to place his arm round her waist?

WINKE.   I am.   (*He glares at* CARVALLO.)   I even suggest that some perfect strangers might achieve that position in less than half an hour.

CARVALLO.   Gross, re-apply the bayonet!

(GROSS *prods* WINKE *with his bayonet*.)

Now, what brought you to this particular spot?

WINKE.   I've told you—I'm a wandering scholar.   I wandered in here.

CARVALLO.   Can you explain the reason for your wearing Mr Darde's clothes?

WINKE.   Yes.   My own got wet in the rain this morning.

CARVALLO.   Did it rain this morning?

WINKE.   Yes.   At eleven o'clock.

CARVALLO.   Did you notice any rain at eleven o'clock, Gross?

GROSS.   No, sir.

CARVALLO (*to* WINKE).   You are lying.

WINKE.   May I cross-examine the witness?

CARVALLO.   Certainly.

WINKE (*to* GROSS).   Where were you at eleven a.m.?

GROSS.   On defaulters.

WINKE.   What reason have you for supposing that while you were on this parade, in company with various other scrimshankers, misfits and petty criminals, it was not raining?

GROSS.   Because I didn't see any rain, nor feel any.

WINKE.   Do you mean to tell this court that you trust the evidence of your senses?

GROSS.   Yes.

WINKE.   Would it, or would it not surprise you to learn that the senses of our species are declared by numerous eminent authorities to be notoriously unreliable?

GROSS.   Yes.   No!   What are you talking about?

WINKE.   Would it or would it not?   Answer me, yes or no!

GROSS.   How can I?   You . . .

WINKE.   The witness is totally unreliable.

CARVALLO.   And so are you.   Your various moral problems

are your own. I am only concerned with military security. I'm afraid, Mr Legion, that I must put you under arrest.

WINKE. In that case may I see you alone?

CARVALLO. If you want to.

<u>GROSS. Clear the court!</u>

(DARDE *and* SMILJA *rise.* SMILJA *exit down* L.)

<u>(*He moves to* R. *of* DARDE *and marches him down* L.) Leff—right—leff—right—leff—right—leff.</u>

CARVALLO. And clear out yourself, Gross.

(DARDE *and* GROSS *exit down* L.)   EXIT

(*Busy with paper work.*)   Well?

WINKE. Simply this. If you put me under arrest, I shall tell Darde that I caught *you* embracing his wife. He is a very jealous man. So you'll not get one glimpse of her for the rest of your stay.

CARVALLO (*looking up*). I don't think I'm interested in her any more. I thought she was an upright woman. I find she's the property of anyone who happens to drop in.

WINKE. I don't understand why you should want her to be an upright woman, when your sole desire is apparently to achieve her downfall.

CARVALLO. For the simple reason that I have a romantic nature. If I were a realist, I should press my attentions on the servant.

WINKE. Then I can promise you that your goddess is quite secure on her pedestal. I got no further than the very innocent embrace you saw.

CARVALLO. Oh. Has she not shown you any signs of affection?

WINKE. None whatever. She is entirely yours.

CARVALLO. Unluckily she's Darde's. All the same, it's my duty to arrest you.

WINKE. I suggest a compromise. Put me on parole until tomorrow.

CARVALLO. I can think of only one good reason why you should so particularly want your freedom for tonight.

WINKE. My dear boy, don't be absurd! From this moment I'm giving up women altogether. I cannot describe to you the countless advantages of a chaste and celibate existence.

CARVALLO. How do you know? You've only tried it for the last five minutes.

WINKE. I can imagine it in the future. Just consider the advantages. One dissipates no energy in the display of one's charms, one shaves or grows a beard, just as one likes; one has a bathroom to oneself and a bed undivided—one has all the advantages of being a monk, with none of the drawbacks of being religious.

CARVALLO. You are condemning married life, and there I entirely agree. But consider the advantages of being a philanderer. One's natural instincts are liberated, not repressed.

WINKE. Just a moment ; we cannot begin to argue until we have defined our terms.

CARVALLO. What the hell are we arguing about, anyway ? I was conducting a Court of Inquiry !

WINKE. I don't know ! You started it.

ENTER

(GROSS *enters down* L.)

GROSS. Excuse me, sir. The lady asked me to take a look at the water.

CARVALLO. It never occurred to you that she probably did so to get a quiet word with her husband ?

GROSS. No, sir, it didn't. And the water's nearly boiling and it's getting on for eleven. How much longer am I to sit in there with them two ?

CARVALLO. I was just concluding my interrogation, Gross. Bring in Mr Darde.

EXIT

(GROSS *exits down* L.)

You know, you're the first decent opponent in an argument I've found since a fifth columnist I shot last October. I hope we shall have a chance to reopen our conversation.

WINKE. I hope so, too.

CARVALLO. Oh, but—there was that little matter of putting you under arrest, wasn't there ? But I'm sure that a man of your intellectual integrity would never break his parole. Consider yourself free for the moment, but report to me tomorrow at eight.

WINKE (*moving* R.C.). That's jolly good of you. Only—being a wandering scholar, I have no bed for the night. If you were to place me under house arrest, old Darde would have to put me up.

CARVALLO. I'll arrange it.

ENTER

(DARDE *and* GROSS *enter down* L. DARDE *crosses to* R. *of the table.*)

HALT @ TABLE

GROSS (*halting* L. *of the table*). Prisoner and escort—halt !

CARVALLO. Mr Darde : Legion is under house arrest. Would you mind putting him up for the night ? I know it's rather a lot to ask.

DARDE. You are asking me no more than is required of all of us : to forgive my enemy. I gladly do so. I have schooled myself through many years of self-discipline to be able to forgive anybody almost anything, in the knowledge that they will surely suffer for the wrongs that they have done me through all eternity in the life to come.

CARVALLO.   That must be most satisfactory.   (*He collects his papers together.*)

DARDE.   My wife's error took the nature of indiscretion, rather than sin.   I have forgiven her also.   We are thus happily re-united, and by showing mercy towards the author of our wrongs we will doubtless re-enlist him in the battalions of the Pure in Heart.

WINKE.   Amen.

CARVALLO (*rising*).   Hear, hear.   This is a most affecting scene.   I've a bottle of brandy in my car—may I ask you all to join me in a little celebration ?

DARDE.   It is against my principles to indulge in strong drink. And it is a double abomination to take it from the hands of one's enemies.

CARVALLO.   The advantage of brandy is that it may be weakened with water according to the strength of one's convictions. (*He moves up* C.)   If you win the war you can call it reparations ; if we win, you can call it an aid to reconstruction.

(*He exits up* C.   GROSS *follows him off.*   SMILJA *enters down* L.)   EXIT

WINKE.   How we got out of that, I really don't know.

SMILJA.   I've explained to Caspar what happened.

WINKE (*to* DARDE).   Really, you're the worst conspirator I've ever met.

(SMILJA *moves to the dresser and picks up her knitting.*)

DARDE.   I do not like being forced by circumstance to tell lies.

WINKE.   You told some pretty stupid ones, I must say.   Why you had to tell him that I was in Velma, I don't know.

DARDE.   How else was I to explain that I had your papers ?

WINKE.   I'm sick to death of pretending to be someone else. I, a materialist, socialist, celibate biologist, have had to pretend within a couple of hours to be a dissenting evangelist and an anarchist seducer.   I'll be heartily glad to be myself again.

SMILJA (*moving to the chair down* L.).   You can't be.   He didn't believe in you from the very first moment he heard of you. He called you " The Improbable Professor ".   (*She sits and knits.*)

WINKE.   It was all caused by your rushing in and jumping to damn fool conclusions when you saw me embracing your wife.

DARDE.   I was not aware that an enemy officer was present. Had I seen him, I should have known you were pretending.

WINKE.   If you had come in quite casually and said that you were me, there would have been no trouble at all.

DARDE.   I've had quite enough of being you.   I find it even more difficult to assume your character than to wear your ridiculous trousers.

WINKE. Damn it all—look at yours on me! And do you realize that tomorrow morning he'll probably take me out and shoot me? I've had to play the most squalid and underhand tricks to keep my freedom tonight, so I can meet this agent fellow and hand him the despatches.

DARDE. Had you not malingered yourself out of your mission, I should not have had to do it for you.

WINKE (*easing* R.). As it turns out, you've had the best of the bargain.

DARDE. I have had nothing of the kind! I was concealed in a stuffy cupboard for nearly three hours—it was highly disagreeable. Were I a younger man, I would have joined the army and fought as an honest soldier. Instead I am made a secret agent, and have constantly to practise the most corrupting deceptions. I can only console myself by recalling the story of the two spies sent by Joshua into Jericho.

(*The* BARON *enters up* C.)

BARON (*moving down* R.C.). I thought I'd never get in without him seeing. I . . . (*He looks from* DARDE *to* WINKE *and back again in great astonishment.*) And I thought I was sober.

DARDE. We had to exchange missions. This is Professor Winke of Velma University.

BARON. Oh. How d'you do?

WINKE. How d'you do?

BARON (*with elaborate casualness*). They say the price of fish will be even higher next year.

WINKE. The price of meat is also mounting rapidly.

BARON. X-Y-Z-two-three-four?

WINKE. R-S-T-seven-eight-nine.

BARON. Good—you're the chap. Have you something for me?

WINKE. Excuse me a moment. It's stitched inside my shirt.

BARON. Good! Congratulations on the successful conclusion of your mission. Now, fresh instructions have arrived.

WINKE (*fumbling inside his shirt*). Oh—really, this is too much!

DARDE. But I have only just got back from a long and tedious assignment.

BARON. May I remind you both that a complaint from more than one party constitutes mutiny? Are you questioning my authority?

DARDE. No.

WINKE. No.

BARON. I'm glad to hear it. Haven't you finished fishing in your underwear?

WINKE. Here it is. (*He takes a paper from inside his shirt and hands it to the* BARON.)

BARON. Thank you. (*He puts the paper in his pocket.*) Now tomorrow is the anniversary of the Foundation of the Republic.

WINKE. Long live the King !

BARON. What ?

WINKE. I mean—Hail to the Republic !

BARON. I should hope so.

WINKE. Sorry—these things change so quickly.

BARON. Instructions have arrived that a gesture is to be made. Every Partisan is expected to kill at least one enemy in honour of the occasion.

WINKE. Oh.

DARDE. Oh. Secure in the righteousness of our cause, we cannot fail. Though I wish we had longer notice.

WINKE. Who are you going to kill ?

BARON. Billeted in my lodge is a Deputy Assistant Paymaster General.

SMILJA. The one I've seen about the village—with a lot of silver braid on his cap ?

BARON. Yes.

SMILJA. But he's quite an old man—with spectacles.

BARON. Whoever I kill is my business. I'm here to see that you carry out yours. Now, is that young officer billeted here ?

DARDE. Yes.

BARON. You can take him. Is there anyone else ?

(SMILJA *rises in horror.*)

WINKE. There's his batman.

BARON. He'll do for you.

DARDE. But what about reprisals ?

BARON. The same thing is being done all over the country. They cannot take reprisals against the whole population.

WINKE. They certainly can. They can decimate us.

BARON. Have you any objection to being decimated ?

WINKE. The very strongest objection. And anyway—a small point of accuracy—you cannot decimate one person ; you can only decimate ten.

BARON. Well, there are only four of us here, so we're perfectly safe. Anyone who fails in his duty is simply letting down the side. This is an operation that requires team spirit, Winke. I shall expect two corpses, then, by noon tomorrow.

WINKE. But . . .

BARON. Yes ?

WINKE. Well, the captain is really rather an engaging young fellow.

BARON. What's that got to do with it ?

WINKE. Since you're asking us to kill him, it seems to me to have everything to do with it.

BARON. Are you suggesting that a soldier, before he shoots, should consider whether his target is an engaging young fellow, or otherwise ?

WINKE. I'm certain that if he did so, he would seldom shoot.

BARON. If you're a pacifist, you should never have joined the Partisans.

WINKE. I only joined to convince future governments of my integrity as a scientist. As a scientist, I fail to see how the evolutionary process will be served by killing the captain. He's a very desirable specimen. If I had my way, I would not make him a corpse, but a donor.

BARON. Suppose this sort of conversation went on between every officer and his troops before an attack. What sort of a state should we be in then ?

WINKE. Utopia.

BARON. If you disobey orders, as soon as the war is over, I'll have you run in for collaboration.

WINKE. Assuming that we win the war.

BARON. Of course we shall win.

WINKE. Why ?

BARON. Because the cause of freedom always triumphs.

WINKE. Explain, then, the prolonged servitude of certain Asiatic peoples.

BARON. Dammit, I will not argue !

DARDE. The Baron is right. It is our duty to smite the unrighteous.

WINKE. For heaven's sake stop talking in that dreadful medieval jargon of yours. By " smiting the unrighteous " I suppose you mean eliminating the anti-social—so for goodness sake say so.

SMILJA. It is quite out of the question that the captain should be killed. I will not have it.

BARON. You shouldn't be here at all—go away. This is a man's affair.

SMILJA. It's nothing of the kind. Some woman went through time and trouble and pain to bring the captain into the world, and all you men can do is to find ways of putting him out of it.

WINKE. After all, he's a guest in this house. We can't abuse the conventions of hospitality.

BARON. He is not a guest. He is a billetee.

DARDE. He demanded accommodation. We can kill him with a clear conscience.

BARON. Of course you can. Thanks for your example, Darde. (*He moves up* C.) And you'll report to me at the castle as soon as you've done it. At least—not immediately—about seven-thirty, when I've had my morning tea. (*At the door.*) And don't forget, if it isn't done to my satisfaction, I'll damn well denounce you for collaboration. And you know what that means ? Purge.

(*He exits up* C.)

SMILJA. Caspar—this is quite unthinkable !
DARDE. Go upstairs to your room.
SMILJA. I won't ! I'll find the captain and warn him.
DARDE. Then I shall be arrested and shot. Would you sooner lose your husband than a stranger ?
WINKE. Mrs Darde, I think it would be better if you went. I will see what I can do.
SMILJA. You promise not to do anything without telling me ?
WINKE. I promise to tell you.

(SMILJA *crosses to the stairs, goes up them and exits.*)

DARDE (*moving to the stove*). Now : let us look at the problem methodically. What ways are there of destroying him ?
WINKE (*moving to* R. *of the table*). Adopting a strictly scientific attitude : strangulation, which subdivides itself into manual or mechanical ; suffocation, by a liquid, a solid, or a vapour ; decapitation, incision, combustion, laceration, explosion or contusion.
DARDE. Or poisoning.
WINKE. I had forgotten poisoning.
DARDE. We might do worse than study the methods revealed to us in the Bible.
WINKE. I agree that the Old Testament is probably the most comprehensive work on the subject.
DARDE. There is little information, so far as I remember, on strangling. There are some hundred and sixty references to burning, excluding those to burnt offerings, but the only relevant one comes, I think, in second Kings, where fire came down from heaven and burnt up the two captains. Perhaps that is too much to hope for. Pharaoh's captains were drowned, and sank to the bottom like stones. Jeremiah talks of breaking captains in pieces, and also of making them drunk. That might be a sound suggestion—to intoxicate him first, so that in his confusion he would be easier to despatch ?

(CARVALLO *enters up* C. *He carries a bottle of brandy.*)

CARVALLO (*moving above the table*). Ah ! We have the most comfortable quarters—I'm really most grateful. Could I borrow a corkscrew and some glasses ?

(DARDE *moves to the dresser.*)

You've no idea of the variety it gives to life to be constantly moving about and sleeping in strange places. One night I'll be in a shell hole, and the next in a disused palace. Oh, but of course—you're a wandering scholar, aren't you? You under-stand all the advantages.

(DARDE *gets a corkscrew from the dresser and puts it on the table.*)

WINKE. I must say, I don't quite understand yours. The price of the varied experience you enjoy is a complete uncer-tainty as to how long you will enjoy it.

CARVALLO. And that very uncertainty makes me doubly grateful for life. (*He picks up the corkscrew and opens the bottle.*)

DARDE. You are not, then, afraid of death? (*He gets the jug of water from the dresser.*)

CARVALLO. I'm afraid of the pain and unpleasantness with which I might die, but I don't think I'm at all afraid of being dead. That is—I'm not afraid of ceasing to exist. But if there's any chance that in some bodiless form one may continue to exist after death—then the prospect is quite terrifying.

DARDE. Why? (*He moves to the dresser and gets three glasses.*)

CARVALLO. Well, if my mind ever has to exist without my body, then there is no prospect of any peace for me at all.

DARDE (*putting the glasses on the table; in great concern*). Do you mean to imply that without the satisfaction of your body's appetite, your mind can never be at rest?

CARVALLO. I'm afraid I do. (*He fills the glasses then sits above the table.*)

DARDE (*drawing the chair down* L. *to* L. *of the table*). But when you have ceased to be flesh, such desires will no longer trouble you. (*He sits.*)

CARVALLO. I wish I could be sure of that. But even though all my bodily passions had been spent, my mind could continue to live on credit.

(WINKE *draws the chair down* R. *of the table closer to it and sits.*)

DARDE. But that is perfectly impossible! (*He drinks.*)

CARVALLO. You don't know my mind. (*He drinks.*)

WINKE. You and he ought to have a talk. When I was pre-tending to be you, he confessed a wish that someone would undertake his conversion. (*He drinks.*)

DARDE. He did?

CARVALLO. Yes. Though I'm a sinner, and clever enough to justify my sins philosophically, sin is like a diet of bread and potatoes: it fills you up for the moment, but never satisfies. In fact, I'm ready and ripe for conversion to some other way of life, though I've no idea what it is. And I shouldn't like to die until I know more about it. (*He drinks.*)

(DARDE *looks from* CARVALLO *to* WINKE.)

DARDE (*extremely troubled*). I have undertaken many con-versions, but none where the case was so particularly urgent.

CARVALLO. I say—I do like talking to you chaps. I haven't let myself go like this for ages. Look! I'm just a bit suspicious that you've been doing something fishy—black market or something—but I feel so comfortable among you that—we'll say no more about it. We've become—well, we've really become friends, haven't we? And though we have to go our own ways and do our various duties, in a personal friendly way we do sort of *trust* one another, don't we?

WINKE. Yes.

DARDE. Yes.

CARVALLO (*refilling his glass*). I was sure you'd feel it, too. Have some more brandy.

WINKE. Thank you.

(CARVALLO *refills* WINKE'S *glass*.)

DARDE. Thank you.

(CARVALLO *refills* DARDE'S *glass*.)

WINKE. I hope the captain will be at least temporarily spared.

DARDE. The same thought had occurred to me.

CARVALLO. For heaven's sake! I'm not going to be killed tonight, am I? The front's fifteen miles away.

DARDE. It is given to no man to foresee the hour when he may be taken. (*He drinks.*)

WINKE. That is my brandy.

DARDE. I beg your pardon. (*He sips his own brandy.*) Though my principles do not allow me to partake of strong drink, I think they would allow my next one to be a very little stronger. Captain Carvallo: I could not undertake to assist you unless I could have you to myself for at least a week. Although I once converted a blacksmith in an hour and a half, he had just seen an angel at the bottom of his garden, and the case was therefore exceptional. If there is no chance of such an arrangement, I'm afraid I shall have to abandon your soul to the Devil, and—send you on your way.

CARVALLO. We are supposed to be resting. We should be here for at least a week or ten days.

DARDE. I see.

CARVALLO. Then will you take me on? I don't promise to become converted to your particular creed, but I'm sure that an intensive course of your views should at least help me to believe in something.

DARDE. I will think about it. But there are—other decisions to be taken first.

(GROSS *enters up* C.)   ENTER

GROSS (*saluting*). Picket commander reports he's ready for inspection, sir. (*He moves to the stove, picks up the pan of water and takes it up* C.)

CARVALLO. Oh, yes. (*He rises.*) Mr Darde, I must say that I'm already predisposed in your favour. The good grace with which you are treating this vagabond robber of women's virtues shows remarkable broadness of mind. (*He drinks.*)

DARDE. I have extended to him nothing more than common charity.

CARVALLO (*moving up* C.). I wish all husbands were as charitable.

(He exits up C., *followed by* GROSS *who carries the pan of water.)*

WINKE. Well ?

DARDE (*rising*). I am exceedingly troubled in my mind. I was glad when the opportunity came for me to join the armies of the righteous and slaughter at least one of the worshippers of Baal—there is no need to flinch at what you call my jargon. In a hundred years' time your own will seem just as old-fashioned. But now I am offered the choice of either slaughtering or saving him. It is clearly better that he should be saved. But will the Baron consent to a postponement, until I have seen whether he is redeemable or otherwise ?

WINKE. I doubt it. There's this question of the anniversary tomorrow.

DARDE. There is no equally suitable anniversary in about a fortnight's time ?

WINKE (*consulting his diary*). Not that I can think of. There's the Feast of St Barnabas—or American Independence Day, some way ahead. Of course what we could do is to make an unsuccessful attempt at killing him ; produce some evidence to show the Baron that we've tried. You haven't any explosive, have you ?

DARDE (*pointing to the cupboard* R.). There are a hundred kilogrammes of ammonal behind some hymn-books in that cupboard.

WINKE. Good ! Now suppose we blow up your stable.

DARDE. What ?

WINKE. You're insured against war damage, aren't you ?

DARDE. I believe so.

WINKE. Well then, suppose we blow up the stable, but arrange for them to be out when we do it ?   The debris will show the Baron that we've tried ; we can blame the explosion on a stray shell, and you'll get a nice new stable when the war is over.

DARDE (*after a pause for consideration*). I will just examine my lease. (*He moves to the dresser.*) And how do we arrange for him to be out of his bed in the middle of the night ? (*He takes a document from the dresser drawer.*)

WINKE. What about having a fire ?

DARDE. You're already exploding the stable, and you needn't think you're going to burn down the house.

(SMILJA *enters by the door at the top of the stairs and comes down.*)

SMILJA. What have you decided to do ?

WINKE (*rising*). We're going to blow up the stable, having arranged for the captain to be out.

SMILJA (*crossing to the stove*). How will you make sure that he's safe ?

(DARDE *moves to* R. *of* WINKE.)

WINKE. That is the problem.

DARDE (*reading the document*). " All that messuage and premises situate and being at or near the village of pom-pom-pom, together with all lights, easements, ways, paths, passages, waters, watercourses, profits, commodities, advantages and appurtenances, pom-pom-pom—shall at his own proper costs and charges sufficiently repair and maintain the said messuage and premises, together with all lights, easements, ways, paths, passages——"

WINKE. Water and watercourses, pom-pom-pom—do for heaven's sake hurry !

DARDE (*reading*). —" and shall peaceably and quietly yield up unto the said landlord at the end of the said term—fire or other inevitable accidents excepted." All is well. (*He moves to the dresser and replaces the document in the drawer.*) Both my capital and my principles are protected. We will do it. Have you thought of a way of ensuring his absence ?

WINKE. There is one solution, but I doubt if you'd approve.

DARDE (*moving above the table*). Let us hear it.

WINKE. We might provide him with an assignation.

DARDE. With whom ?

WINKE. A woman.

DARDE. Your suggestion is shameful in the extreme. What woman ?

WINKE. We've only got two—your wife, and Anni.

DARDE. It would be perverting the girl's mind. I will not hear of it.

WINKE. We haven't time to argue ! Let Anni make an appointment with the captain, and then you can tell him to-morrow how wicked he was to accept. It would make an excellent prologue to his conversion.

SMILJA. You are both forgetting the batman.

DARDE. I have noticed no signs of regeneration in *him*. He must be blown up.

WINKE. It would add realism. But it does seem a pity.

SMILJA. I think you're planning all this extremely badly. Anni is not nearly experienced enough to deceive the captain, and it might have a most dangerous effect on her.

WINKE. What do you suggest ?

SMILJA. I suggest that you leave the captain to me.

DARDE. What ?

SMILJA. That *I* should make an assignation with him.

DARDE. But—but you're a married woman ! You're middle-aged—you're a respectable housewife—don't be ridiculous—he'd laugh at you.

SMILJA. I think, all the same, that I could keep him out of the stable for as long as you require.

DARDE. Oh—if he's as bad as that, then he's not worth saving.

WINKE. My dear fellow, what man invited by your wife to a rendezvous could possibly refuse ?

DARDE. Eh ?

WINKE (*hastily*). I except myself, of course, because I've particular principles on the subject. But believe me, no normal, young, unattached bachelor-at-arms of any country would turn down such a chance unless he were—well, unless he were good, which normal young men simply are not, for excellent biological reasons.

DARDE. The whole idea strikes me at once as a shameful offence against common morality, and a gross abuse of the sanctity of family life. Where would the meeting take place ?

WINKE (*after a relieved nod to* SMILJA). It can't be outside because he'd see us firing the charge. It can't be in here, because the window overlooks the stable. It will have to be in a room that looks the other way.

DARDE. There is only one room that does, and that is the bedchamber, and that is absolutely unthinkable.

SMILJA. I do not think it unthinkable.

DARDE. What !

SMILJA. Surely the salvation of the captain's soul is of more importance than some slight risk to my reputation ?

WINKE. Don't you see ? She invites him upstairs. He agrees. As soon as he's turned that corner, we set off the explosion. He probably won't even see her.

DARDE. But where am I, while all this is occurring ?

SMILJA. You will have to go away for the night.

DARDE. What ! I will not !

WINKE. You need only pretend to.

SMILJA. Drive away in the trap, turn out the horse at the bottom of the lane, and creep in by the back way.

WINKE (*moving in to* R. *of* DARDE). The whole plan is perfectly arranged.

SMILJA (*moving in to* L. *of* DARDE). With a perfect alibi for Caspar.

WINKE. It's completely foolproof.

SMILJA. The nice captain is saved.

WINKE. And the horrible Baron satisfied.

DARDE. I feel very strongly indeed that . . .

WINKE.   We knew that you would agree !

SMILJA.   Of course we did !

WINKE.   Congratulations on your courageous decision !

DARDE.   Oh, very well—I will do it.   But it occasions me grave perturbation of conscience.

WINKE.   Good.   Get out your explosive.   (*To* SMILJA.) You fetch a large trunk.

(SMILJA *exits down* L.)

DARDE (*crossing to the cupboard* R.).   Will you give me some assistance with the hymn-books, please ?   (*He opens the cupboard and starts to take out some bundles of hymn-books.*)

WINKE.   Can't you do it yourself ?   (*He crosses to* R.)   I ought to keep watch.

DARDE.   There are a hundred and forty, tied in bundles of ten.

WINKE (*helping with the bundles*).   If you hadn't taken so long to make up your mind the whole thing would be done by now. Why are they getting bigger ?

DARDE.   Those are the choir copies.

WINKE (*heaving bundles*).   I know—that if a certain—stimulus —is applied—to a certain sort of man—he'll behave in a perfectly predictable manner.   On that assumption I can plan.   You bog yourself down in ethics—and dogma—and medieval dialectic. For heaven's sake—how many more are there ?

DARDE (*sticking his head out of the cupboard*).   Five.   And part of a harmonium.

WINKE.   I don't know what's the use of your precious freedom of action when you're so inhibited you can hardly act at all.

DARDE (*re-appearing with a harmonium keyboard*).   This is not the time for a debate on First Principles.   Please be careful of the bindings.

(SMILJA *enters down* L. *dragging a small trunk.*)

WINKE.   Is the coast still clear ?   You know, I'm ashamed to admit it, but I do feel a certain boyish exhilaration.   " Beware of the Black Hand, or blood will spill !   Ha-ha-ha-ha-ha ! "

(SMILJA *drags the trunk* R.C. *then runs to the window up* R.)

DARDE.   You are being absurd—and you're trampling upon my Apocrypha !

WINKE.   I'm sorry.   (*To* SMILJA.)   Can you still see him ? (*He opens the trunk.*)

SMILJA (*at the window*).   Yes.   No—no.   He's coming back !

WINKE.   Quick—where's the explosive ?

SMILJA.   He's coming up the path—oh, hurry !

DARDE (*handing out the tins of explosive*).   Here !

WINKE.   Help pile it in the trunk.   Oh—look out—for God's sake be gentle! If we meet him this is your luggage—you understand? You're going to Velma. (*He takes the tins from* DARDE *and puts them in the trunk.*)

DARDE. Another dissimulation required of me!

WINKE (*to* SMILJA). And don't forget you're to make an assignation with the captain—upstairs, and as soon as possible.

SMILJA. I'll do everything I can.

DARDE. Don't do more than you need!

SMILJA. He's coming in! (*She runs to* L. *of the trunk.*) He's just outside—he's wiping his boots!

DARDE. I knew it! I knew we would be discovered! (*He shuts the cupboard door and with the last tin in his hand moves below the trunk.*)

WINKE. Shut the trunk! Sit on it!

DARDE. I can't—this one won't go in.

WINKE. Then hold it—go on—sit on the trunk. (*He snatches a hymn-book and stands* R. *of the trunk.*)

(DARDE *closes the trunk and sits on it with the tin on his knees.*)

(*He sings.*)*

" There is a joyful shore
Far, far, far above."

(DARDE *and* SMILJA *join in the singing.* CARVALLO *and* GROSS
enter up C.)

" Where saints and sinners join
In righteousness and love."

(CARVALLO *stands to attention* R. *of* GROSS *and nudges him to do likewise. After a moment, he snatches off* GROSS'S *cap and thrusts it in his hand.*)

" O, O, O, O to be
Among that blessed band,
And dwell in ecstasy
Within that Promised Land."

ALL. Aa-men.

CARVALLO (*moving to* R. *of the table*). I must apologize for interrupting your devotions.

WINKE. That's quite all right. Mr Darde has been suddenly called away, and we were just having a little service to give him a good send off. (*He drops the book on to the pile.*)

CARVALLO (*looking at the hymn-books*). You seem to have been expecting rather a large congregation?

(SMILJA *eases up* C.)

* The music for this hymn is given on page 70.

WINKE. We were helping old Darde to pack. He has to go to Velma for the night.

CARVALLO. Not bad news, I hope?

DARDE (*rising*). No. I have to see my aunt.

CARVALLO. But I thought you had buried her this afternoon?

DARDE. So I did.

CARVALLO. Well, how can you see her?

WINKE. The coroner has given instructions for her instant exhumation.

CARVALLO. Oh—for a post-mortem? Is foul play suspected?

WINKE. I'm afraid it is. And for all we know, it may be old Darde who's done it. Now, come on, old chap—time to make a start.

(DARDE *and* WINKE *pick up the trunk and manœuvre it to the door up* C. SMILJA *hands* DARDE *his hat from the hooks and in taking it, he drops the trunk. They pick it up with great anxiety.*)

SMILJA (*kissing* DARDE). Have a safe journey.

(GROSS *opens the door up* C.)

DARDE. I thank you. And may you be safely delivered from the perils of the hours of darkness.

(WINKE *and* DARDE *exit up* C., *carrying the trunk between them.*)

CARVALLO. Well, I don't think there's anything else, Gross. Call me at six-thirty.

GROSS. I suppose you've forgotten you were going to have a bath? It'll be practically cold again by now.

CARVALLO. Oh yes, so I was. I'll be along in a moment. Good night, Gross.

GROSS. Good night, sir.

(He salutes and exits up C., closing the door behind him.)   E X I T

CARVALLO (*taking cigarettes and matches from his pocket*). I don't suppose you smoke, do you?

SMILJA (*moving down* R.C.). No, thank you.

CARVALLO. Do you mind if I do?

SMILJA. Not a bit.

CARVALLO (*after lighting a cigarette*). I feel dreadfully ashamed.

SMILJA. Why?

CARVALLO. An hour ago . . . Well, I'll make a clean breast of it. I tried all the old tricks on you because I thought that what I felt for you was only a passing fancy. I realize now that —shall I say that this is something quite different from the usual hail and farewell? That my accustomed sense of humour about these matters has quite deserted me, and I find myself desperately, ludicrously serious?

SMILJA. You are lucky to be able to compare what you are feeling with what seem to be innumerable other occasions. I can't do so, because I've never experienced anything like this before.

CARVALLO.   I'm so glad—and I do hope you're enjoying it.

SMILJA.   No, I'm not.

CARVALLO.   Look, as one of the tricks of the trade I told you a lie tonight.   I said I might have to leave tomorrow.   In actual fact I'll probably be here for at least a week or ten days.   I shall be able to spend plenty of time with you, shan't I ?   I would so like to walk in the country with you—take you for picnics in the car.

SMILJA.   I'm afraid I don't think that will be possible.

CARVALLO.   But it must be !   I can't stay here so near you, and never see you alone.

SMILJA.   But my husband will be here and I have meals to cook.

CARVALLO.   When does he come back ?

SMILJA.   Tomorrow morning.

CARVALLO.   So we have only a few hours of tomorrow without him ?

SMILJA.   Yes.   Only a few hours of tomorrow.   And of—tonight.

CARVALLO.   Tonight ?

SMILJA.   Yes.

CARVALLO.   You—you're suggesting that . . . I don't think that you quite understood me just now, when I said that my attitude had changed.   Really, this is desperately difficult to explain, but—my intentions towards you are—now—entirely honourable.

SMILJA.   Oh.

CARVALLO.   I know I may seem inconsistent, but—please believe me—I ask nothing more than—just to be with you ;   to talk about—oh, to talk about all the things we like and the things we hate, and—to sit side by side and feel terribly sad that nothing more is possible.   And all this, don't you see, depends upon my knowing beyond all doubt that you are completely and eternally unattainable.

SMILJA.   Oh dear—everything has gone wrong !

CARVALLO.   Wrong ?   Everything has gone right !   Your husband was going to try to convert me to some better way of life—a week, he said, was the least time he needed.   But you have converted me in less than an hour, without argument or dogma—simply by being what you are.

SMILJA.   Nevertheless, one must be practical !

CARVALLO.   Practical !   Have I made some ridiculous mistake ?   Oh, but it serves me right !   I fall properly in love for the first time in my life, and I find myself loving a woman who wants to treat me in just the same way as I've always treated women.

SMILJA. Look: couldn't we meet just for a little while tonight—to be alone, and talk, and—and—read poetry to one another ?

CARVALLO. But we *are* alone. We *are* talking. I have the selected works of Victor Hugo in my pocket.

SMILJA. Then—it's no use my saying any more.

CARVALLO. No. Please understand : I'm trying to pay you the greatest compliment a man can pay to a woman.

SMILJA. I believe it's supposed to be ; though at the moment I can't quite see why. But surely—circumstances—time—make it madness—to deny ourselves so obstinately. It is really, now I come to think of it, a little selfish of you.

CARVALLO. I have heard exactly the same arguments used by my sex to yours. Especially the one about selfishness.

SMILJA (*in utter exasperation*). Oh !

(WINKE *enters up* C.)

WINKE. Ah, hullo ! Well, I've seen Darde off. (*He yawns elaborately.*) Oh, it's getting late, I think I'll turn in. Where am I to sleep ?

SMILJA. You'd better have the sofa in the parlour.

WINKE. Thank you. I shall sleep like a log tonight—the Crack of Doom wouldn't wake me. It's a beautiful night outside.

" And Spring's shy scent still lingers on
    To grace maturer summer's charms ;
Who on a night like this would not
    Desire the girdle of thy arms."

By the way : don't take too much to heart what I said about living without women. I only suggest that ten per cent of the world should live my way, and you, I can see, are far more suited by temperament to the other. (*He moves to the door down* R.) I wish you joy of it. Good night !

CARVALLO. Mr Legion—a point of etiquette : as we are two single gentlemen in the presence of a lady whose husband is absent, and as the hour is late, I think it would be more seemly if we both retired simultaneously. The lady's reputation will thus not be compromised by either of us. (*He moves to the door up* C.)

WINKE. Oh—a very delicate suggestion. Are you ready to withdraw ?

CARVALLO (*holding the handle of the door up* C.). Perfectly.

WINKE (*holding the handle of the door down* R.). One, two, three.

CARVALLO ⎫
WINKE   ⎬ (*together*). Good night !

(CARVALLO *exits up* C.   WINKE *exits down* R.   SMILJA *moves to the table and for the first time in her life, pours out a full glass of neat brandy and drinks it.*   WINKE *re-enters down* R.)

Well ?

SMILJA.   He won't come.

WINKE.   *What ?*

SMILJA.   He absolutely refuses.

WINKE.   This is disastrous !   You must have played your cards extremely badly.

SMILJA (*tearfully*).   That is quite possible.   I have no experience of the game.

WINKE.   How did you set about it ?

SMILJA.   I pointed out, as tactfully as I could, that the opportunity existed.

WINKE.   Wrong !   Utterly wrong !   Good heavens, didn't you see that the man is a romantic ?   A romantic is a person who can't be persuaded to do anything until he's convinced that there's no possible chance of succeeding.

SMILJA.   Well, I wish you'd made your suggestions before I had to take part in your stupid plan.   I've had to behave like a —like a *loose* woman—demean myself in front of him.

WINKE.   But that's what was wrong.   You ought to have *exalted* yourself in front of him.

SMILJA.   Can you tell me how to exalt yourself and offer yourself at one and the same time ?

WINKE.   No, I can't !   But I imagine every experienced woman has the trick.

SMILJA.   I am not an experienced woman.   And then you turn round and—and blame me and bully me.   I . . . (*She dissolves into tears.*)

WINKE.   Oh, what the blazes is the matter now ?   (*He crosses* R. *of* SMILJA.)   Oh, do stop—I've no idea what to do with you.   *Stop it, will you !*

(SMILJA *cries louder.*)

(*He leads her to the chair down* C.)   Now, really—honestly—I didn't mean to offend you.   Now, sit down, and I'll see if I can find you a handkerchief anywhere, and . . .

(SMILJA *sits in the chair down* C.   DARDE *enters down* L.)

Oh—there you are !

DARDE.   Here, indeed, I am.   And it seems to me that whenever I step over my own threshold, I find you with your arms round my wife.

WINKE (*moving* R.).   Oh—now don't be ridiculous !

SMILJA (*rising*).   Don't be so silly, Caspar.

WINKE.   The cause of the crisis is that the captain has refused an assignation.

DARDE. He has ? Then I am infinitely more optimistic of his salvation. But why does that make her weep ? Anyone would think she were disappointed.

WINKE. You made some unpleasant remarks about her appearance. Now that the captain has turned her down, she thinks they must have been justified, and her pride is naturally hurt.

SMILJA (*moving to the window up* R.). It is *not* my pride ! (*She draws the window curtains, then moves to the other windows in turn and closes the curtains.*)

DARDE. I should hope not. And I did not make unpleasant remarks. I said that she was middle-aged and respectable. Am I to understand, then, that the attitude in which I found you was one of comfort and succour, and not, as I assumed, of libidinous importunity ?

WINKE. Yes. No. I mean—the former.

DARDE. Then I apologize.

WINKE. That's all right—I forgive you.

DARDE. Thank you—I had already forgiven myself. Now : I have driven with some ostentation down the lane, and luckily I was seen by the batman. That establishes the fact that I am no longer here.

WINKE. Good. Now, we have to think of some other way of getting the captain out of bed.

SMILJA (*peering through the curtain*). There's no need to, because he isn't in it.

WINKE. What ?

SMILJA. He's leaning over the orchard gate and looking at the moon—in the most stupid and silly and effeminate attitude.

WINKE. Can he see the stable from where he is ?

SMILJA. No.

WINKE. We're saved ! Or rather, he is. Turn out the lamps—and open the front of the stove to give us some light. (*To* SMILJA.) You go up to your room. Darde—slip out by the back way and stand by that fuse. (*He turns out the table-lamp.*)

(DARDE *opens the front of the stove and a bright red glow fills the room.* SMILJA *goes up the stairs and exits.*)

DARDE. I am somewhat inexpert at handling explosives. I'm sure that with your scientific training . . .

WINKE. Don't argue. (*He moves to the window up* R.) Have you some matches ?

DARDE (*moving to* L. *of* WINKE). There's a box in my pocket.

WINKE. Well, give it to me, then.

DARDE. I did not say your pocket—I said mine.

WINKE. What ?

DARDE. I said *my* pocket—which is in my jacket on you.

WINKE. What in the . . . Oh, I see. (*He takes a box of matches from his pocket and gives it to* DARDE.) Now, stand by. And when you're to light the fuse, I'll strike a match in this window—clear ?

DARDE. When I'm to light the fuse, you will light a match in this window.

WINKE. Yes.

DARDE. Yes.

WINKE. And look out for the batman. He may not be in bed yet.

DARDE. I earnestly hope he is. (*He moves down* L.) I would like to destroy at least one of the unrighteous before the Armistice.

WINKE. He's much more likely to be unrighteous if he's not in bed. (*He peers through the curtains.*) It's all right—the captain's still there. If I don't light the match, you'll know it's because he's either gone up to bed, or is hanging about in the danger area. Go on—quickly ! You take so much time over everything.

(DARDE *exits down* L. WINKE *peers through the curtains.* DARDE *re-enters down* L.)

What the hell have you come back for ?

DARDE. To give you a match to strike in the window.

WINKE (*crossing to* R. *of* DARDE). Anyone with any sense would have thought of that before.

DARDE (*giving* WINKE *some matches*). I would like to point out that . . .

WINKE. Go on !

(*He bundles* DARDE *off down* L. *then returns to the window up* R. SMILJA *enters at the top of the stairs. She carries a lighted candle.*)

SMILJA. What's happening ?

WINKE. Go back to your room !

SMILJA. But I want to know what's happening.

WINKE (*peering through the curtains*). The captain is still looking at the moon. Your husband is on his way to the stable to fire the charge. You'd hardly believe it, but he's stopped to do up his bootlace.

SMILJA. Please let me come.

WINKE. No ! We've quite enough to attend to, without a lot of women messing up our lines of communication. Go to bed.

(SMILJA *exits at the top of the stairs.* WINKE *opens the curtain of the window up* R. *and is about to strike his match, when he suddenly sees something outside. He looks frantically around for a hiding place, then hurries to the cupboard down* R., *enters it and closes the door.* GROSS *enters quietly up* C. *He wears plimsolls. He listens for a moment, closes the door, then tiptoes to the table and helps himself to a drink from the bottle of brandy. He stifles a choking fit, then tiptoes towards the stairs. There is an audible click from the latch of the door up* C. GROSS *stops suddenly, looks around for a hiding place, then hurries to the cupboard down* R., *enters it and closes the door.* CARVALLO *enters cautiously up* C. *As he closes the door, there is a gasp from the cupboard down* R. GROSS *emerges in a panic and runs to the door up* C.)

CARVALLO (*in a furious whisper*).   Gross !   What the hell are you doing in here ?

GROSS.   I—I—I came to get that bottle of brandy in case you'd forgotten it.

CARVALLO.   You're a liar.   You're after that servant girl.

GROSS.   All right—I am.   But there's something bloody awful in that cupboard.

CARVALLO.   What do you mean ?

GROSS.   I hid in there when I heard you coming in, and I put my hand—on a face.

CARVALLO.   A face ?

GROSS.   A human face.   It never moved—but it was still warm.   If you ask me, someone's hanged himself.

CARVALLO.   Well, we'd better investigate.

GROSS.   Yes, sir.

CARVALLO.   Have you a weapon ?

GROSS.   No, sir.

CARVALLO.   You should have.   Your instructions are that you should never leave quarters unarmed.

GROSS.   Tonight I wasn't expecting much resistance.

CARVALLO (*moving down* R.).   Fetch me the poker.

(GROSS *gets the poker from beside the stove and hands it to* CARVALLO.)

Now—you open the door.

(GROSS *gingerly opens the cupboard door and peers in.*)

(*He peers into the cupboard.*)   There's a shocking smell of brandy —and I think there's something in that corner.

GROSS.   Give it a poke, sir.

(CARVALLO *pokes into the cupboard.   There is a yelp and* WINKE *hurriedly emerges.*)

CARVALLO.   What on earth were you doing in there ?

WINKE.   If it comes to that, what the devil are you two doing in a private house at close on midnight ?

CARVALLO. I'm sorry to say that my servant had absented himself without leave, and was on an errand of love.

WINKE. And what are you doing?

CARVALLO. I was apprehending him.

WINKE. I don't believe you.

CARVALLO. Old chap, we know each other fairly well by now. I can say—for your ears alone—that biology was too strong for me.

GROSS. Huh!

CARVALLO. I beg your pardon, Gross?

GROSS. I was going to say, sir—for your ears alone—that I can understand some words of more than one syllable.

WINKE. Could you possibly lend me a cigarette?

(CARVALLO *gives a cigarette to* WINKE *who moves to the window up* R.)

CARVALLO (*to* GROSS). There's an old adage, Gross, which says, " Like Master, like Man ".

(WINKE *strikes a match and waves it in the window.*)

But in case anyone should think that you have been corrupted by my example, I should like to put it on record that when you were batman to the Padre, you behaved, if anything, worse than you do now. (*He turns and moves up* R.)

(WINKE *hurriedly turns from the window and lights his cigarette.*)

WINKE. Well, you're a fine pair, I must say. However, as it happens nothing could have turned out better.

CARVALLO. Why?

WINKE. I mean—that Mr Darde is away, and I'm an easy-going chap who sees, hears and speaks no evil.

CARVALLO. That's extremely good of you.

WINKE. Not at all.

CARVALLO. But—might I just ask exactly why you were hiding in that cupboard?

WINKE. I—I am sorry to say that biology proved too strong for me, also.

CARVALLO. You! You were on your way to her—after all you said?

WINKE. I am terribly afraid so.

CARVALLO. It hurts me dreadfully to have to tell you that she made an assignation with me somewhat earlier this evening. I'm afraid I have the prior claim.

WINKE. No doubt, as the years go by, I shall cease to feel it so profoundly.

CARVALLO. This situation, Gross, is shockingly bad for discipline.

GROSS. I was just thinking that myself, sir. I'm setting you a very bad example.

CARVALLO. Don't forget you've to call me at half past six.

GROSS. No, sir. May I go now, sir?

CARVALLO. Yes.

GROSS (*saluting*). Thank you, sir. Good night, sir.

CARVALLO. And don't salute without your hat on.

(GROSS *goes upstairs and exits.*)

WINKE (*moving to the door down* R.). Well, things being as they are, I think I'll retire to my sofa.

CARVALLO. That situation was embarrassing all round. But I think, being men of intelligence and good taste, we could all justify our behaviour philosophically?

WINKE. I can think of at least three modern philosophical systems which would assure us all that we're behaving like positive saints.

(*He exits down* R. CARVALLO *looks at himself in the mirror, takes a book of poetry from his pocket, opens it, selects a poem, then goes upstairs and exits.* WINKE *re-enters down* R., *looks at his watch and paces up and down. After a few moments a slight noise is heard off down* L. WINKE *moves to the arch down* L. *and looks off.*)

What are you doing in there?

(DARDE *enters down* L.)

Have you lit it?

DARDE. Yes.

WINKE. Well—make yourself scarce. You're supposed to be in Velma.

DARDE. I can't stay outside.

WINKE. You must.

DARDE. I won't. (*He pushes past* WINKE.) Allow me to take cover.

WINKE. Don't be so stupid—it's only a small charge.

DARDE (*getting under the table*). We may have miscalculated the force of the explosion.

WINKE. Possibly. (*He rapidly joins* DARDE *under the table.*)

DARDE. What has happened? I saw two figures come in at the door.

WINKE. It was the captain and the batman.

DARDE. What?

WINKE. The captain is now with your wife, and the batman is with Anni.

DARDE. Oh, monstrous iniquity! They are not worth saving —either of them. That fuse is a long time burning.

WINKE. How much was there?

DARDE.   Two and a half metres.

WINKE.   It should have gone up by now.   You're sure you lit it properly ?

DARDE.   Yes.   It went fizz, and burned with an offensive odour.

WINKE.   It must have gone out.   Go and see what's happened.

DARDE.   I will not !   It would place me in a most dangerous situation.

WINKE.   Need I remind you of your wife's situation ?

DARDE (*rising and moving to the dresser*).   I disliked this plan of yours from the very first.   (*He takes a book from the dresser drawer.*)

WINKE.   What are you doing ?

DARDE.   Finding my manual on explosives.   (*He opens the book and refers to it.*)   Demolitions, page twenty-two.   (*He reads.*) " Action in the event of the charge failing to explode : on no account leave cover for at least twenty minutes."   (*He returns hastily under the table.*)   I cannot wait here for twenty minutes.

WINKE.   Well, if you can't trust your wife for twenty minutes, you must just take the risk and go out with a new match.

DARDE.   Very well, I will.

WINKE.   That's a good fellow.   And give me the newspaper, will you ?

DARDE.   I console myself with the assurance of the Prophet Isaiah, that the faithful shall walk through the fire and not be burned.

WINKE.   In that case, you may as well stand upright.

DARDE (*rising and moving down* L.).   Faith does not imply a lack of common prudence.   How much time has elapsed since I lit the fuse ?

WINKE (*rising and moving to* L. *of the table*).   Six minutes.

DARDE.   As much as that !   If I do not return, tell my wife to put my savings in the National Bank of Switzerland, and my mortal remains—fragmentary though they may be—in plain unvarnished pine.   My funeral is to be arranged by the Velma branch of the Co-operative Society—and please remind my wife to draw the dividend.   Tell her I went to my death to save her honour . . .

WINKE.   If you don't go quickly, there'll be none to save.

DARDE *exits quickly down* L.   WINKE *looks at his watch, glances up the stairs then gets the newspaper from off the cupboard up* L. *and a cushion from the chair above the table.   He gets under the table and settles down to make himself comfortable.   The sound of a tremendous explosion and the clatter of falling masonry is heard off* L.   WINKE *leaps to his feet in horror as—·*

the CURTAIN *falls.*

ACT III

SCENE.—*The same. The early hours of the next morning.*

When the CURTAIN *rises,* DARDE *lies on a couch set* R.C. *His clothes are tattered and torn.* WINKE *is putting the final knot in a bandage around* DARDE'S *head. The stove is closed and a pot of coffee stands on it. The window curtains are closed and the table-lamp is lit.*

WINKE (*moving to the dresser*). Would you like a cup of coffee? (*He takes two mugs from the dresser, moves to the stove and fills the mugs with coffee.*)
DARDE. Of the sons of Kohath; Uriel the chief, and his brethren an hundred and twenty. Of the sons of Merari; Asaiah the chief, and his brethren two hundred and twenty. Of the sons of Gershom; Joel the chief, and his brethren an hundred and thirty. Or was it two hundred and thirty?
WINKE (*looking at his watch and glancing up the stairs*). I've no idea. Would you like some coffee? (*He puts one cup on the table, moves to the dresser and gets the bottle of aspirin.*)
DARDE. Of the sons of Elizaphan; Shemaiah the chief, and his brethren . . .
WINKE (*moving to* DARDE). Oh, do shut up for goodness' sake!
DARDE (*tearfully*). I cannot remember. I cannot remember the number of the sons of Elizaphan.
WINKE. You'd better have some more aspirin. (*He gives* DARDE *two tablets.*) Here you are.
DARDE. Two white pills. Why do you keep requiring me to swallow two white pills? (*He puts the tablets in his mouth.*)
WINKE. They are a sedative, and you're suffering from shock. (*He gives the coffee to* DARDE.)
DARDE. Their taste is bitter in my mouth. (*He sips some coffee.*) Is it Monday or Tuesday?
WINKE. Friday.
DARDE (*returning the mug to* WINKE). Has the hay been cut?
WINKE. No.
DARDE. No? Then I must see to it—it ought to have been in a fortnight ago—what are they thinking about, not to have cut the hay?
WINKE (*moving to* R. *of the table*). Do please keep calm, shut up and relax. (*He puts the mug on the table.*) I wish to heaven I had some morphia for you. It preserves the sanity of the

nurse as much as the health of the patient. (*He drinks his own coffee.*)

(*A rumble of gunfire is heard in the distance.*)

DARDE. What was that?
WINKE. Guns, I think.
DARDE. The war. Yes—the war. Where is my wife?
WINKE. She's upstairs.
DARDE. Why does she not come down? (*He continues mumbling, and eventually goes to sleep.*)
WINKE. That's just what I'm wondering. (*He moves below the table.*) They say that love is blind. Apparently it's stone deaf also.

(CARVALLO *enters at the top of the stairs.*)

CARVALLO. Oh—oh, good Lord—what's happened? (*He comes down the stairs.*)
WINKE. Mr Darde, returning from the somewhat macabre spectacle of the exhumation of his aunt in Velma, was blown up by a stray shell. He is now suffering from shock.
CARVALLO (*moving* C.). I see. I had not expected him to come back until very much later.
WINKE. That might be inferred from your behaviour.
CARVALLO. Is he . . . ?
WINKE. He is not, luckily for you, in a condition to appreciate what has been going on. There is one thing that puzzles me ; did you or did you not hear a perfectly distinct explosion at about five past twelve last night?
CARVALLO. Yes. I did.
WINKE. Then you might have had the decency to come down and investigate. For all you knew, I might have been injured.
CARVALLO. You forget that I'm an army officer, and *ex officio* a gentleman. As an officer, I'm quite accustomed to loud bangs in the night, and I take no notice unless I'm sent for. As a gentleman, I do not desert a lady who seems to be finding my company agreeable.
WINKE. Then—she didn't *insist* on your deserting her?
CARVALLO. Not at all. Indeed, she allayed any anxieties I might have had by saying the explosion was caused by a delayed action bomb in the orchard they had been expecting to go off for some time.
WINKE. Well, really!
CARVALLO. So we continued to talk, and read Victor Hugo aloud to one another.
WINKE. Is that what you've been doing?
CARVALLO. Yes.
WINKE. From midnight until twenty-past four?
CARVALLO. Yes.

WINKE. Do you expect anyone to believe you?

CARVALLO. No. Not anyone. But a sensitive person who understands these matters would believe and understand me perfectly. There can be such a thing as a beautiful friendship.

WINKE. Only before lunch. Not in the small hours.

CARVALLO. You're a low prurient fellow—I've a damn good mind to knock you down! All this piffling propaganda of yours about chastity is simply a mask to cover up a private life of unparalleled sensuality. Dammit, if you don't believe me, I *will* knock you down! Do you believe me, or not?

WINKE. Faith, they say, is often a by-product of fear: and your fist under my nose is a very persuasive evangelist. If you removed it, I might be able to think reasonably.

(CARVALLO *relaxes his aggressive stance.*)

M'm. Yes—I think I do believe you. But how do you propose to explain your beautiful friendship to Darde?

CARVALLO. That is one of those practical matters that one never considers until after breakfast.

WINKE. Well, you may be interested to know that the explosion you heard blew up your quarters and everything in them.

CARVALLO. What?

WINKE. Whether it was caused by a stray shell, a jettisoned bomb, or some of those villainous Partisans from the hills, I wouldn't know.

CARVALLO (*moving to the door up* C.). I must go and investigate this. (*At the door.*) By the way, as I caught you in that cupboard last night, it's obvious that we're tarred with the same brush. I think we might agree on a conspiracy of silence, don't you?

WINKE. I certainly do. I have a reputation to keep up.

CARVALLO (*suddenly suspicious*). What reputation?

WINKE. The—the reputation of a wandering scholar.

CARVALLO (*on his guard*). I see.

(*He exits up* C.)

DARDE (*opening his eyes*). I have a distinct impression of something being wrong.

WINKE. That is the usual reaction of anyone returning to the world of the living. I've no doubt it's the first sensation of new-born babes—with quite good reason.

(GROSS *enters by the passage at the top of the stairs.*) ENTER

GROSS. Oh—what on earth . . . (*He comes down the stairs.*)

DARDE. A face I seem to know. Are you aware, young man, of the number of the sons of Elizaphan?

GROSS (*moving* C.). Is he cuckoo?

WINKE. Very possibly—in both senses of the word.

GROSS. What's happened to him ?

WINKE. He's been blown up by a stray shell. So has your billet.

GROSS. What ! Was that the bang I heard in the night ?

WINKE. Yes.

GROSS. I was told it was a dud shell in the hen run.

WINKE. That had been expected to go off for some time ?

GROSS. Yes.

WINKE. The fertility of a woman's imagination is astonishing. Your captain is outside investigating.

GROSS. Oh. Look—I need a bit of help. I'm thinking of going absent.

WINKE. Deserting ?

GROSS. Well—yes. I—I want to marry young Anni.

WINKE. Oh. Does she want to marry you ?

GROSS. She says so. She behaves like it.

WINKE. Have you any—interests in common ?

GROSS. Yes.

WINKE. That is an interest which everyone has in common. I mean, have you a mutual interest in Art, or gardening, or sport, or philanthropy, or something ?

GROSS. I haven't really had time to find out.

WINKE. What are your own interests ?

GROSS. Ever since I was a boy, I've been in the army. My favourite occupation has been avoiding doing my duty.

WINKE. As most of the duties required of you were probably perfectly senseless, that shows remarkable uprightness of mind. But are you capable of doing your duties as a husband ?

GROSS. Eh ?

WINKE. Marriage was ordained for three purposes. For the prevention of fornication—though in your case it's a little late in that respect. For the procreation of children—which seems anyway an inevitable process among the lower income groups ; and for the mutual society, help and comfort that the one ought to have of the other.

(CARVALLO *enters up* C. *and stands peering at the floor.*)

GROSS. Strewth. When it comes to religion, you're as bad as the old geyser himself.

WINKE. Like most atheists, I take religion very seriously. I read my Bible daily, and divert myself on journeys by exploring the byways of the prayer book.

(CARVALLO *licks his finger, presses it on the floor, and examines it. Stooping every few paces, he makes his way to the cupboard down* R. GROSS *moves up* C. *and stands to attention.*)

CARVALLO. H'm !

WINKE. What's the matter?

CARVALLO. The Partisans in this neighbourhood are very skilful.

WINKE. Why?

CARVALLO. They managed to get unseen into this house last night, and they took their explosive to blow up my billet from this cupboard. The explosive used was ammonal. It's a yellowish powder—not unlike lemonade crystals. One of the containers must have had a hole in it, because there's a trail of the explosive all the way from this cupboard to the ruins of the stable. Mr Legion : is it possible that you have been trying to blow me up?

WINKE. No—no—— I assure you . . .

CARVALLO (*moving* C.). Last night, I thought of you as a decent fellow ; a low, lecherous sort of fellow, of course, but still an honest one. I liked and trusted you enough to put you on parole. And half an hour later you tried to blow me up in my bed. It's no use looking at Mr Darde—he was away, exhuming his aunt in Velma. Or was he? Ah, yes! This aunt of his, I take it, was an alibi? And the stray shell a miscalculated explosion. It's a cold morning. You had better both get your coats.

WINKE. Where are we going?

CARVALLO. To headquarters—under arrest.

WINKE. But Darde is a sick man—you couldn't be so heartless.

CARVALLO. Heartless! When you sat here last night drinking the brandy of a man you had planned to blow up? I see that the heart is a superfluous organ, when dealing with the people of your country. Fetch your coats.

WINKE. Captain : I see that there is only one thing I can do —to tell you the truth.

CARVALLO. In the last eight hours you have told me, with a perfect semblance of truth, that you were Caspar Darde, farmer and lay-preacher, and Primus Secundus Tertius Legion, a wandering scholar, whose character has varied from an irreclaimable lecher to a reformed rake and back again. As a matter of interest, what are you now?

WINKE. I am sorry to say that I am really and truly the improbable Professor Winke.

CARVALLO. Who lends out clothes in Velma? Quite. Gross, march them off.

WINKE. Please—give me one minute's free speech. Then I'll go where you want.

CARVALLO (*looking at his watch*). Very well—sixty seconds from now.

WINKE. Mr Darde and myself are both Partisans. Last night we had instructions from our headquarters to murder you and your batman. We didn't want to kill you, because—well, frankly, I liked you and found you a lively opponent in an argument ; and Darde wanted to save your soul before you met your Maker. So we arranged to blow up your quarters, which would show our superiors that we'd tried, but we also arranged for you to be absent when we did so. Thus, you are alive, and we are apparently good enough patriots to be lay-preachers and biologists when the war is over.

CARVALLO. You know, your stories have a kind of brilliant improbability which makes it seem quite impossible that anyone could make them up. You say that you arranged for me to be absent. You did nothing of the kind. I happened to be—out of the way, because I had made an assignation with—he is asleep, isn't he ?—with his wife.

WINKE. I admire your chivalry, Captain. But the fact is, that Mrs Darde made an assignation with you.

CARVALLO. How do you know that ?

WINKE. Has it not occurred to you that we might have arranged that too ?

CARVALLO. Then . . . On your word of honour, is this true ?

WINKE. On my word of honour, yes.

CARVALLO. So that all she said last night was just—pretending ? I can't believe it ! Do you mean to say that he was prepared to sacrifice his wife's reputation in exchange for the salvation of my soul ?

WINKE. Not quite. We thought that when you heard that explosion, you would certainly—descend. The story of the unexploded bomb would seem to show a certain sincerity in the lady's dissimulation which we had not allowed for.

CARVALLO. I am absolutely confused—I . . . It's all right, Gross, you can stand easy.

(GROSS *relaxes*.)

WINKE. Confused ? Why ?

CARVALLO. Is she in love with me ? Or was she only saving my life ? And—if she doesn't love me—was my life worth saving ? He *is* still asleep, isn't he ?

WINKE. Yes.

(GROSS *moves above the couch and peers at* DARDE.)

CARVALLO. He's not dead, is he ?

WINKE. No.

CARVALLO. He risked his life, and his wife's reputation, to save me. Now had I behaved like a gentleman, I would have come down when I heard that bang to see if anyone was hurt. Instead, I stayed upstairs.

WINKE. Reading Victor Hugo.

CARVALLO. Oh! I've been playing in a bedroom farce, while all the rest of you were playing drama.

WINKE. Tragedy.

CARVALLO. Tragedy. (*He looks quickly towards* DARDE.) Is he all right, Gross?

GROSS. Yessir.

CARVALLO. If you hadn't blown up my revolver, I would here and now cheerfully blow out my brains.

DARDE (*waking suddenly*). Two hundred! It was two hundred!

CARVALLO. What?

DARDE. The number of the sons of Elizaphan. It was two hundred.

CARVALLO. I'm quite sure you're right. (*To* WINKE.) What the hell is he talking about?

WINKE. He's delirious, and he ought to be in bed. Will you give me a hand?

CARVALLO. Certainly. It is the very least I can do. Gross— things sound rather lively outside. You'd better get the wireless from the car.

(GROSS *exits up* C. CARVALLO *and* WINKE *move to* DARDE *and start to lift him.* SMILJA *enters at the top of the stairs.*)

SMILJA. Caspar! Caspar—what's happened to him? (*She runs down the stairs.*)

WINKE. Oh, it's all right. The poor old chap was only blown up by that explosion, which you may or may not have heard at midnight last night.

SMILJA. What—then . . .

WINKE. Don't worry—I'm a qualified doctor as well as a biologist. Shock and multiple contusions—that's all.

(DARDE *burst suddenly into the hymn:* "*There is a joyful shore.*")

CARVALLO. I'm sure this is awfully bad for him.

WINKE. Try saying "Amen".

CARVALLO. Amen.

(DARDE *instantly stops singing.* WINKE *and* CARVALLO *carry* DARDE *up the stairs and exit.*)

SMILJA (*calling*). Anni! Anni—come quickly! (*She opens the window curtains and lets in the daylight.*)

(ANNI *enters at the top of the stairs.*)

ANNI. Yes, Mrs Darde. (*She comes down the stairs.*)

SMILJA (*putting the kettle on the stove*). Bring up this water when it's hot—and make the coffee. (*She puts out the table-*

lamp.) It's nearly milking time and the cowherd will want his breakfast.

(*She goes up the stairs and exits. There is much rumbling of gunfire outside.* ANNI *puts the ham, some knives and forks and crockery on the table.* GROSS, *with a wireless receiver slung on his chest, enters up* C.)

GROSS.   There's merry hell going on through these earphones. Sounds as though the whole army was talking at once.   Here— all right if I have a slice of ham ?

ANNI.   You can if you want to.

(GROSS *moves above the table*.)

GROSS (*carving*).   Thanks.   Look—one of the troubles about girls is that they always give you the cold shoulder the next morning—as though it was all your fault.   I've never known a case yet where it wasn't six of one and half a dozen of the other.   So don't stand there looking down your nose at me. Apart from anything else, it isn't the sort of nose you can look down, 'cos it turns up at the end.

(CARVALLO *enters by the door at the top of the stairs and comes down*.)

CARVALLO (*moving to* R. *of* GROSS).   Anything audible on the air, Gross ?

GROSS.   I should say there is.   I can't make it out.

(ANNI *moves to the stove*.)

CARVALLO.   Let's listen.   And cut me a slice of ham, will you ?   (*He takes the wireless from* GROSS, *listens through the earphones, and his expression changes*.)

GROSS (*carving*).   There isn't a flap on, is there ?

CARVALLO.   They're giving the emergency codeword.   The unit's on the move.   The whole front must be on the move. (*He picks up the mouthpiece to speak*.)

GROSS.   They'll—they'll come to see what's happened to us, I suppose.

CARVALLO.   They won't need to.   We must get back at once. (*Into the wireless*.)   Hullo, Juno three, hullo, Juno three . . .

GROSS.   Sir !

CARVALLO.   What ?

GROSS.   We've known each other for a long time, sir.

CARVALLO.   Whenever you say that, it always means that you're going to ask for something impossible.   What is it ?

GROSS.   Has it occurred to you, sir, that our billet is flat ?

CARVALLO.   Yes.

GROSS.   Then where are we ?

CARVALLO.   Here.

GROSS. How does anyone know ?

CARVALLO. Are you suggesting we desert ? I've a damn good mind to put you under arrest !

GROSS. Well, look at it this way, sir : if we'd been in bed last night, we'd be goners. If we go up the line, we'll probably be goners. Why be a goner when you needn't go ? I want to get into civvies and marry Anni.

CARVALLO. Don't be ridiculous, Gross. You've never wanted to marry them before. What's come over you ?

GROSS. Love.

CARVALLO. What do you propose to do after you've married her ?

GROSS. There's a shocking shortage of manpower. The farmers'll give anything for a cowhand. All right, sir. If your mind's made up, speak to H.Q. Tell them you're on your way, and ask for a lance-corporal and escort to arrest me.

CARVALLO (*into the wireless*). Hullo, Juno three, hullo Juno . . . (*To* GROSS.) Gross, this is most unfair. You know that my mind's in a most unsettled state this morning. The men in this house have gone to astonishing lengths to avoid killing me. Can I now go up the line and repay them by turning the fire-power of my company on their fellow citizens ? (*He puts the wireless on the table.*)

GROSS. That's the spirit, sir—no, you can't ! Let's get into civvies, sir, and beat it.

CARVALLO. It's all very well for you. You can marry that girl and become a cowhand. But I've no prospects at all. I've always found that doing my military duty still allowed me to behave in my private life with complete absence of scruple or responsibility. But if I'm to do my duty now, look what it is. I must arrest you for attempted desertion ; I must shoot old Darde and the improbable Winke for being Partisans, and report Mrs Darde for aiding and abetting them. And I must go and fight in what sounds like an elaborate battle at just the time when I want to sit and think.

GROSS. You sit and think, then. But—is it all right if I push off ?

CARVALLO. Perhaps the best way in which I can reward your long and faithful service is by showing you on the casualty return as missing, believed killed.

GROSS. I appreciate that, sir. (*He turns to look at* ANNI.) All right then ?

ANNI. I don't mind.

(GROSS *winks, clicks his tongue and exits down* L.)   EXIT

CARVALLO. How very simple life is for you. It's all right with him—you don't mind. (*He clicks his tongue as* GROSS *did.*)

ANNI. I don't see what else there is to it.

E

CARVALLO. You're very fortunate.

ANNI. It's extraordinary how it clears things up for you. Yesterday I was worrying about what sort of a person God is, and what sort of a person I am, and all sorts of things were in a whirl and a muddle in my head. Now I don't have to worry about them any more. I shall wash his clothes, and cook his meals, and slap his children, and be far too busy to worry about anything except the housekeeping. But I wonder what I shall say when my daughter's nineteen and asks me the sort of questions I asked Mrs Darde ? Perhaps I'll just be honest and say that, like most other women, after I got married I stopped thinking.

(WINKE *enters at the top of the stairs. He wears the same clothes, but his own hat. He carries the brief-case and umbrella.* ANNI *titters.*)

WINKE (*coming down the stairs*). I suppose that now I look even more improbable than ever ?

CARVALLO. You certainly do. (*He moves to the window up* R. *and glances out.*)

WINKE. I've saved my political reputation at the expense of an excellent suit of clothes. One of your troops has arrived on a bicycle. He's looking at the ruins of the stable.

CARVALLO (*moving to the stove*). Would you do me a favour ? I promise this time not to abuse it. Will you go and tell that man that a stray shell landed on us last night, that you dug in the rubble and found no sign of life ?

WINKE. I shall never have broken bad news with more gladness.

(WINKE *exits up* C. ANNI *pours out two mugs of coffee and exits with them down* L. CARVALLO *warms himself at the stove.* SMILJA *enters at the top of the stairs and comes down to* R. *of the table.*)

CARVALLO (*after a pause*). The professor is telling my orderly that I'm dead.

SMILJA. What are you going to do ?

CARVALLO. I'm deserting. I—I thought I might try to find some work around here—as a civilian.

SMILJA. No—no—you mustn't do that.

CARVALLO. Why not ? Don't you want to see me any more ?

(SMILJA *breaks* R.C.)

You asked me to—meet you last night—as part of a plan to save my life.

SMILJA. Yes.

CARVALLO. Then—the plan went wrong.

SMILJA (*turning*). Everything went wrong. We must now—
put things right again.

CARVALLO (*moving to* L. *of* SMILJA). Why? Why?

SMILJA. Listen. In every person's life, however strict their
upbringing, there comes a chance to forget themselves as they've
become, and do some wicked, wonderful thing that perhaps is
wrong enough to undo all the good they've ever done. Or perhaps is the only thing to make their life worth living . . . To
you, I was only one of a series of events . . .

CARVALLO. No—no, you weren't . . .

SMILJA. If I wasn't, I soon shall be. But to me, you were—
that magical event I've been talking about. Now, it's over.
And whatever you decide to do, I must never see you again.

CARVALLO. I can't hope to convince you that you were the
same to me as I was to you?

SMILJA. If I could only think that . . . (*She turns her face
quickly away.*)

CARVALLO. Then?

SMILJA. You will have made me very happy—but you must
still go.

CARVALLO. I see.

SMILJA. We've behaved so dreadfully that I can't believe—
if we went on seeing one another—we'd be allowed to be happy
any more.

CARVALLO. Allowed! Who allows these things—or forbids
them?

SMILJA. That's something you should have been taught when
you were young. If you ever find the answer for yourself, I
think you'll understand me—as I, now, understand you. What
I didn't know before was the strength and the beauty of the
thing that's forbidden. You've taught me that.

CARVALLO. So, everything that we mean to one another,
instead of dying tragically or gloriously, must just—peter out,
like the stump of a candle in a saucer?

SMILJA. That's the way things do die. Flowers, love, people
—even soldiers, if you watch them instead of reading about
them.

(WINKE *enters up* C.)

WINKE (*moving to* L. *of the table*). Well, I've convinced him for
you. He was very sad about it, and he stuck up two bits of
wood in the shape of a cross, so at least you've had a Christian
burial.

(*A growing rumble of gunfire and the sound of aircraft is heard off.*)

CARVALLO. Thank you. But I don't think that, after all, it
was necessary.

WINKE. Why?

CARVALLO. I haven't the courage to begin a life in which I'd have to think everything out from the beginning all over again. There are times when habit, discipline, routine, are the only medicines to save us.

WINKE. It looks as though something big is brewing up out there. There are planes all over the sky—a great cloud of smoke over Velma.

CARVALLO (*moving to* R. *of the table*). Danger is sometimes a useful stimulant. (*He picks up the wireless, and slings it over his shoulder.*) Sweet and glorious it is to die for one's country.

WINKE. It is not! It's sordid—wasteful—imbecile! So long as we go on pretending it's sweet and glorious, we'll go on doing so in every generation. (*To* SMILJA.) You helped to save his life last night. Are you going to let him walk out and be killed in what may be the last battle of the war?

SMILJA (*turning her back to them*). He would be disloyal to his own comrades if he did anything else.

WINKE. That's the very worst of it. He would be.

CARVALLO. As a biologist, you must have heard of the praying mantis, who eats her mate alive? Once she's used him, there's no further reason for his life.

SMILJA (*turning*). Thank you. It makes it much easier to say good-bye when I know that you're capable of saying things like that.

CARVALLO. Would you say something equally unpleasant to make it easier for me?

SMILJA. Shall I say that you're too wicked and too affected ever to fall in love, so love for you is always unattainable? And being, as you say, a romantic, only the unattainable attracts you. And so you are in love with love as much as you're in love with yourself?

WINKE. Excuse me, but I'm still here. Might I ask, assuming that you survive this battle, what you will do after the war?

CARVALLO. I think I shall become a regular soldier. The life suits me.

WINKE. You will spend your working hours killing men, and your spare time killing animals. You must be mad.

CARVALLO (*moving below the table*). I was born of a mad world. (*He holds out his hand to* WINKE.) Good-bye.

WINKE (*ignoring* CARVALLO's *hand*). Has the comic possibility occurred to you that in the execution of our duty we might shortly be required to shoot at one another?

CARVALLO. You were required to kill me last night, but you didn't.

WINKE. I thought, like Darde, that you were worth saving. Well, I was wrong. Next time I shall kill you without a qualm. I never say good-bye, because it means " God be with you,"

and I don't believe in God.   So I'll say—farewell.   Though I
hope you don't.

(SMILJA *moves to the window up* R. *and picks up* CARVALLO'S
geranium.)

CARVALLO.   Farewell, then.   (*He moves up* C.)   And strangely
enough, I hope you do.   Both of you . . .

(SMILJA *hands the geranium to* CARVALLO *then turns from him
and moves down* R.C.   CARVALLO *exits up* C. *into the growing
sunlight.*   GROSS *enters down* L.   *He now wears peasant clothes.*
He carries his uniform.)   ENTEI

GROSS (*putting his uniform on the table*).   A-milking we will
go—a-milking we will go !   They say out there that you're short
of staff.   All right if I stay on as apprentice milkman, acting
unpaid on probation, and marry Anni as soon as I'm making a
living ?
SMILJA.   You had better be paid at once and marry Anni
immediately.   Otherwise people will start looking at the calendar.
GROSS.   Suits me.   Suits Anni.   Hope it suits the cows.

(*He exits down* L.)   EXIT

WINKE.   I far prefer him to the captain.   The captain was a
scoundrel.   (*He moves to* L. *of* SMILJA.)   Don't worry your head
about him.
SMILJA (*turning from him*).   The scoundrels are the people
one does worry about.
WINKE.   Yes.   (*He cannot see her face.   Just for a moment he
might be going to put his hands on her shoulders, then he turns
and moves up* C.)   I must go, or my tadpoles will be turned into
frogs before I get back.   (*He opens the door up* C.)   Oh—
damnation !
SMILJA (*turning*).   What is it ?
WINKE (*moving above the table*).   Here's Captain Carvallo—in
twenty years' time.

(*The* BARON *enters up* C.   *He wears his haversack.*)

BARON (*moving down* C.).   Ah—good morning !   And a jolly
good one it is, too—have you heard ?   A colossal attack on the
whole front by the Allies !   (*To* WINKE.)   Now, have you and
Darde achieved your objective ?
WINKE.   Yes.   The captain and his batman are no more.
We blew them up in the stable.
BARON.   Oh, jolly good show !
WINKE.   How did you get on with the Paymaster General ?
BARON.   Um—well—sh !   (*He opens his haversack, and shows
a silver braided cap.*)
WINKE.   You killed him ?

BARON. Well, no. Unluckily, he rose too early, and departed in rather a hurry. But he left *this* on a peg behind his door.

WINKE (*indicating* GROSS's *uniform*). Would you like this, too?

BARON. I say—a complete kit! Don't you want it? I would be most grateful. I'll hang it up in my hall—between the lion and the giraffe.

WINKE. In the meantime, sir, may I dismiss?

BARON. Certainly—so sorry—didn't realize you were still on parade.

WINKE (*to* SMILJA). Thank you for all your hospitality.

SMILJA. It's been a pleasure to know you. Good-bye.

(*Very gravely,* WINKE *salutes the* BARON, *then exits up* C.)

BARON. Ah—I think I smell coffee. Your husband up yet?

SMILJA. He was injured last night by the bomb they used to blow up the stable.

BARON (*with a trace of hope*). Seriously injured?

SMILJA. No.

BARON. Oh. Well, at least it means that he won't be down for a day or two?

SMILJA. I'm afraid it does.

BARON (*moving in to* L. *of* SMILJA). Because, early in the morning though it is, you know what I've always felt about you, don't you? I mean—it's not a passing fancy, or hail and farewell sort of thing.

(SMILJA *turns away and cries quietly to herself.*)

It's—well, it's a feeling I've never had in my life before. I'm terribly serious about it, and I wanted to tell you that I . . . (*He turns her to face him and sees that she is crying.*) Good Lord —I say—what's the matter?

SMILJA (*breaking from him*). What? Oh, nothing's the matter. (*She moves up* C.) I'll make you some fresh coffee.

She puts on her apron, and crosses to the stove as—
the CURTAIN *falls.*

FURNITURE, PROPERTY
AND LIGHTING PLOTS

NOTE : The bedroom door which is just visible in the photograph at the top of the stairs, and which has been drawn on the ground Plan to agree, is not necessary to the action of the play. All that is required is a suggestion of stairs leading to the upper rooms.

FURNITURE AND PROPERTY LIST

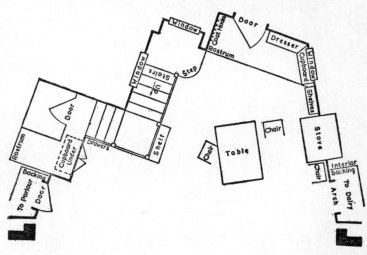

Exterior Backcloth

Throughout the play:

On Stage.—Table. *On it :* oil-lamp.
        Large elbow chair. *On it :* cushion.
        Small elbow chair. *On it :* cushion.
        Small chair.
        Rush mat.
        Dresser. *On it :* plates, mugs, bowls, jugs, cruet, 3 glasses,
                jug of water, aspirins.
                In dresser drawer : knives, forks, corkscrew, docu-
                      ment, book.
        Cupboard (*up* L.). *On it :* bowl of flowers, newspaper.
                In it : plate with ham, platter with bread,
                      plate with cheese.
        Tiled stove. *On it :* cooking-pot, kettle.
        On shelves over stove : cooking and kitchen utensils.
        3 pairs casement curtains.
        3 pelmets.
        Plants in pots.
        Coat-hooks (*up* R.). *On them :* jackets, aprons, etc.
        On shelf R. : battery-type wireless.
        Mirror (R.).
        Bookshelves with books.
        Cupboard (*under stairs*). *In it :* bundles of hymn-books,
                     harmonium keyboard, tins.
        Under stairs up R., *as dressing :* farm baskets, water jars.
        Bundles of onions and herbs.
        Poker by stove.

ACT I

Set.—*Under stairs :* small jar of water.
    On hooks : ANNI'S coat.
    Under cushion on chair L. : knitting.

Doors closed.
Windows closed.
Window curtains open.
Oil-lamps out.

Off Stage.—Broom (ANNI).
    Basket of gooseberries (SMILJA).
    Shotgun (BARON).
    Haversack. *In it :* rabbit (BARON).
    Portable bath (GROSS).
    Military equipment (GROSS).
    Geranium plant in canvas bucket (GROSS)
    Bed linen (SMILJA).
    Packet of cigarettes (GROSS).
    Pan of water (WINKE).
    Brief-case, umbrella (DARDE).

Personal.—WINKE : matches.
    CARVALLO : matches, handkerchief.

ACT II

Strike.—Rabbit, gooseberries and dirty plates from dresser.

Set.—*On table :* documents, forms, writing paper, fountain pen, ashtray.
    On hooks : DARDE'S hat.

Move.—Knitting from table to dresser.
    Chair from L. of table to above it.
    Chair from below stove to down L. of table.
    Chair from R. of table to down R. of it, with an additional chair
      beside it.

Doors closed.
Windows closed.
Window curtains open.
Oil-lamps lit.

Off Stage.—Rifle and bayonet (GROSS).
    Bottle of brandy (CARVALLO).
    Small trunk (SMILJA).
    Lighted candle (SMILJA).

Personal.—CARVALLO : cigarettes, matches, book of poems.
    WINKE : paper inside shirt, diary, matches, watch.
    GROSS : plimsolls.

ACT III

Set.—Couch at R.C.
    Pot of coffee on stove.
    Kettle on floor by stove.
    Close stove.
    SMILJA'S apron on hooks.

Windows closed.
Window curtains closed.
Table-lamp lit.

Off Stage.—Wireless receiver (GROSS).
Brief-case, umbrella (WINKE).
Haversack. *In it :* silver braided cap (BARON).

Personal.—CARVALLO : watch.

There is a joy-ful shore, For far far far a - bove Where saints and sinners join in right-eous-ness and love O, O, O, O, to be a - mong that blessed band and dwell in ecs - ta - sy ——— With-in that prom-ised lane. A - men

LIGHTING PLOT

Property fittings required :
    Fire in stove, practical.
    Table Oil-Lamp, practical.

Interior. The same scene throughout.
The Main Acting Area is C. and L.C.

ACT I

Early evening. Summer.

The Apparent Sources of Light are windows R. and L. The stove is alight
    Outside the windows the sun is setting.

    Cue 1.   WINKE : You know that he was to be sent on a mission.
                                              (Page 7)
                Slow check of all lights. Fade out daylight on backcloth.
                Bring in moonlight.

    Cue 2.   SMILJA lights table-lamp.   (Page 9)
                Bring up lights C. Bring in lamp.

ACT II

    To Open.   Lights as at end of Act I.

    Cue 3.   WINKE puts out table lamp.   (Page 47)
                Check light C. and L.C.

    Cue 4.   DARDE opens stove.   (Page 47)
                Bring up fire glow.

ACT III

    To Open.   Lights as at end of Act II with addition of table-lamp L.C.
                Stove is closed.
                Early morning daylight outside windows.

    Cue 5.   SMILJA opens curtains   (Page 59)
                Increase all lights, follow on with sunrise outside windows.
                      Finish with full daylight at end of act.

    Cue 6.   SMILJA turns out table-lamp.   (Page 59)
                Take out oil lamp.